KU-266-337

Copenhagen

- A in the text denotes a highly recommended sight
- A complete A–Z of practical information starts on p.102
- Extensive mapping on cover flaps

Berlitz Publishing Company, Inc.
Princeton   Mexico City   London   Eschborn   Singapore

Original Text:	Vernon Leonard
Photography:	Jon Davison
Cover Photo:	Courtesy of the Danish Tourist Board
Editors:	Alan Tucker, Stephen Brewer
Layout:	Media Content Marketing, Inc.
Cartography:	GeoSystems Global Corporation

*Although the publisher tries to insure the accuracy of all the
information in this book, changes are inevitable and errors may
result. The publisher cannot be responsible for any resulting loss,
inconvenience, or injury. If you find an error in this guide, please let the
editors know by writing to Berlitz Publishing Company,
400 Alexander Park, Princeton, NJ 08540-6306.*

ISBN 2-8315-7044-1

Revised 1998 – Third Printing November 2000

Printed in Italy

030/011 RP

CONTENTS

Copenhagen

THE CITY AND ITS PEOPLE

In spite of its small size, Denmark has more than its fair share of attractions. A verdant landscape and sleepy villages, beautiful castles, half-timbered cottages, some spectacular beaches, and long stretches of coastline—it's not surprising that Hans Christian Andersen gained so much inspiration from the land of his birth.

Situated at the gateway to Scandinavia, Denmark shares many of the characteristics of its Nordic neighbours: liberal welfare benefits coupled with a high standard of living, and a style of government that aims at consensus and the avoidance of petty bureaucracy. Yet Denmark is also more "European" and accessible than the rest of Scandinavia, and its appeal is universal.

The country consists of 450 islands—at the last count—97 of them inhabited. The only link with the Continent is the peninsula of Jylland (Jutland) that juts up rather like a finger from northern Germany and dominates the country, in area if not in population. With only five million inhabitants, Denmark is still by far the most densely populated Scandinavian country (though not the most populous); the figure of 291 people per square mile dwarfs neighbouring Sweden's 46.

Three ice ages have moulded the gently undulating landscape, which has been transformed into a succession of neat model farms where every barn and farmhouse seems forever freshly painted. Grassland and wheat fields sweep down to the roadside, while white medieval churches with distinctive step-gable towers rise above the village skylines. If you are anticipating any snowy peaks you'll be disappointed. The country's highest hill, Yding Skovhøj, "soars" to a mere 197 metres (568 feet).

Ancient Viking graves at Lindholmhoeje, on the Jutland peninsula.

Like their most famous ancestors, the Vikings, today's Danes are an ebullient and outgoing people, and are also the warmest and cosiest of hosts. Entertaining friends in the home, surrounded by fine furniture, and sitting down to a beautifully-set table well-laden with choice food and drink, is one of the cherished ideals of Danish life.

The consumption of good food is a national obsession among the Danes. Amazing displays of open sandwiches (*smørrebrød*) and possibly the world's tastiest pastries (*wienerbrød*) have to be seen to be believed. The profusion of delicatessen-type salads, cheeses, and fresh fish is as tempting to the eye as to the palate.

As for shopping, porcelain, pewter, and silver goods of the finest quality are manufactured here, and the Danish concept of functional yet aesthetically pleasing design is noticeable in most goods, from household appliances to toys.

Centre of the country's government, administration, and finance, the capital city of Copenhagen is home to 1.5 million people, nearly a third of Denmark's total population. It boasts the oldest royal dynasty in Europe, now headed by Queen Margrethe II and her French-born husband, Prince Henrik.

Broad highways cut swathes through the city. Away from these routes, however, Copenhagen retains a well-preserved old-town area of winding cobbled streets, stuccoed houses, and curio shops, as well as a network of canals. A fairyland quality pervades the city, with its 17th-century green copper roofs and domes, the legacy of Denmark's builder-king, Christian IV.

Crown jewel of this city of pleasure and imagination, the incomparable Tivoli lies right in the centre; more than a fun-fair, more than a park, it's a unique institution near to the hearts of all Copenhageners.

A strong sense of fantasy and colour fills the atmosphere in Copenhagen. Postmen wear bright red jackets and ride yellow bicycles. Chimney-sweeps pass by wearing black top-hats, using them to carry their lunchtime *smørrebrød*. Buses drive merrily along with red-and-white Danish flags fluttering on each side of the cab.

Well before the phrase was sung by Danny Kaye, Copenhagen was known to be "wonderful, wonderful"—a clean, green city full of gaiety, culture, and charm, with a tradition of tolerance and humour. If Hans Christian Andersen were able to return, he would most probably still feel at home here today.

Copenhagen is a place of many colours and surprises: here, an aerial view of the city.

A BRIEF HISTORY

Well before the Vikings organized themselves into an extraordinary nation of seafarers, Denmark was inhabited by hunting peoples. Prehistoric relics of all kinds—some dating back to 50,000 B.C.—abound in Copenhagen's museums and the surrounding countryside, among them Stone-Age flint arrowheads and knives of expert craftsmanship. The oldest surviving costumes throughout all of Europe have been found in this area, as have various musical instruments, including over 30 examples of the famous Danish *lur,* which emits hoarse notes that seem strangely out of keeping with the long, graceful S-shaped stem characteristic of the instrument.

Viking Age

The first written records of the Vikings appear around A.D. 800, at which time Viking raids on neighbouring European countries were becoming notorious. At their peak, these fearless warriors had reached Newfoundland, were rounding the North Cape, and would make sallies to England, Holland, France, Spain, the Mediterranean, and even as far as the Caspian Sea. Prime examples of their boats are on display at the Roskilde Viking Ship Museum (see page 75), and an exca-

---

Holger the Dane

The Viking Holger lived in the early ninth century. He travelled abroad and came back to Denmark in a time of trouble to help fight the country's enemies. Legend has it that he never died, but just went to sleep, waking whenever Denmark was threatened. During World War II, a section of the Resistance adopted the name of Holger Danske. There is a famous statue of him in the Kronborg Castle at Helsingør (see page 70).

---

vated settlement at Trelleborg in West Zealand bears evidence of a camp capable of accommodating nearly 1,300 warriors.

Danish raids upon England gathered in strength during the late tenth century and the first years of the 11th century, culminating in a full attempt at conquest. Canute (Knud) the Great, after meeting considerable resistance, finally became king of England in 1016. The union was to last until 1042.

Egeskov Castle, a Romantic fortified manor, was built in 1554 on the island of Funen.

Christianity had been introduced into Denmark in A.D. 826 by a Benedictine monk, and received the royal seal of approval in 961 when King Harald Bluetooth was converted by a monk named Poppo, who convinced him by seizing red-hot irons in his bare hands. A runic stone set up by Harald at Jelling in East Jutland records that he had "won for himself all Denmark and Norway and made the Danes Christians."

Medieval Times

In 1157, Valdemar I, styled the Great, came to the throne. He leaned heavily on the influence of Bishop Absalon of Roskilde, and this proved a partnership of critical importance to Copenhagen, then just a little fishing village called Havn. With its fine harbour on the Sound (*Øresund* in Danish)—that waterway between Denmark and Sweden which forms the main entrance to the Baltic—the village found itself well-placed on what was becoming one of the main trading routes of medieval Europe.

War-hero as well as statesman, Bishop Absalon fortified Havn by constructing a castle on its small harbour island of Slotsholmen in 1167; this is now acknowledged to be the founding date of the modern city. The name Havn became Køpmannæhafn ("merchants' harbour") in 1170, and eventually København. Today, Slotsholmen lies at the heart of the city. The impressive Christiansborg parliament buildings now occupy the site, but you can see some remnants of Absalon's castle in their cellars (see page 55).

In the course of the reign of successive 12th-century kings, Denmark sorely overextended itself in all directions, and for this it paid dearly in the 13th and 14th centuries. It had interfered in the government of Schleswig and Holstein (the dispute over these two border provinces lasted into the 20th century) as well as troubling the growing trade of the North German Hanseatic ports. So the Germans marched into Jutland. The Danish aristocracy seized the opportunity to curb the powers of its monarchy, and in 1282 King Erik V was forced to sign a Great Charter under which he would rule together with the nobles in the Council of the Danish Realm (Danmarks Riges Råd).

Nevertheless, Valdemar IV Atterdag (c.1320–1375), probably the greatest of medieval Danish kings, led the country back on to a path of conquests and into new conflict with its Nordic neighbours—setting a pattern that was to last intermittently for centuries.

Denmark's hand was greatly strengthened when Valdemar's daughter, Margrete, married Håkon VI, King of Norway and Sweden. After his death, Margrete succeeded through the Treaty of Kalmar in 1397 in unifying the three Nordic powers under her nephew Erik VII of Pomerania. Indomitable Margrete ruled in his name, but was struck down by the plague at the peak of her power in 1412.

HISTORICAL LANDMARKS

50,000 B.C.   First evidence of human habitation in Denmark.

A.D. 800   The first written records of the Vikings emerge.

961   Christianity becomes the official Danish religion with the baptism of King Harald Bluetooth.

1016   Canute (Knud) the Great made King of England.

1167   Bishop Absalon fortifies Havn, thus laying the foundation for the modern city of Copenhagen.

1282   Erik V signs Great Charter, curbing the monarchy's power.

1340   Valdemar IV accedes to the throne; strengthens the country through a succession of conquests.

1397   Treaty of Kalmar unifies Nordic powers—Denmark, Norway, and Sweden—under Danish Queen Margrete's nephew, Erik VII of Pomerania.

1479   Christian I founds university at Copenhagen, confirming the city as Denmark's cultural capital.

1596   Christian IV, the "Great Builder," becomes king and presides over a period of great expansion.

1660   King Frederik III proclaims himself absolute monarch; Copenhagen is made a free city.

1728, 1795   Two massive fires devastate the city.

1801   Danish fleet destroyed in Copenhagen during attack under the command of Admiral Nelson.

1901   Denmark's first democratic government elected.

1914–18   Denmark remains neutral during World War I.

1940   Denmark invaded by Hitler's forces, but a strong resistance movement grows, paving the way for rapid post-war reconstruction.

1949   Neutrality abandoned; Denmark joins NATO.

1972   Denmark becomes a member of European Union (then European Economic Community).

1992   In a referendum, over 50% of Danes reject the Maastricht Treaty on European union.

1996   Copenhagen named "Cultural Capital of Europe."

During the later, true reign of Erik VII (1412–1439), Copenhagen was enlarged. The city then became the official Danish capital under Christopher III of Bavaria in the 1440s; when a university was founded by Christian I in 1479, it also became the country's cultural centre. By this time, the city's population had increased to about 10,000, Schleswig-Holstein was again under Danish rule, and a castle was being built at Helsingør (the Elsinore of Shakespeare's *Hamlet*) to enforce the payment of Sound tolls, for control of the Sound was vital to Denmark's strategic strength at the crossroads of the Northern Seas. Dues were exacted from each ship passing through the 3-km- (2½-mile-) wide channel between Helsingør on Zealand and Helsingborg in Sweden—the channel where ferries cross peacefully every few minutes these days.

By then Denmark stood in a very strong position. Forests had been cleared; new towns and villages had mushroomed everywhere. The scene was set for a turbulent period of 200 years marked by civil war against the nobles, the advent of the Lutheran movement in Denmark, and more wars to come with Sweden.

The Reformation

In the 16th century, with the unprecedented spread of ideas, the latent, deep-seated discontent regarding abuses within the Catholic Church began to be brought out into the open. In Denmark, Catholic bishops had long been putting their wealth to political and military uses, and it was left to Christian III, who reigned 1534–1559, to break their stranglehold. He declared himself supreme authority of a State Church based on Lutheranism, which had made deep inroads since arriving from Germany. The bishops were imprisoned until they "consented," their wealth commandeered to pay royal debts and train new pastors.

Meanwhile, the wars with Sweden lurched on disastrously, with fortunes turning in the favour of the Danes' enemies. By the latter half of the 17th century Denmark had been forced to relinquish her remaining Swedish possessions and to cede also the east bank of the Sound to Sweden. This crucial waterway was now split down the middle, jointly controlled by the two Scandinavian powers, and remains so to this day.

As Denmark licked its many 17th-century war wounds, the city of Copenhagen was given two great consolations. It was made a free city in 1660 in acknowledgement of its bravery during a two-year blockade by Sweden. This meant that all residents were accorded the same privileges as the nobles. Secondly, under Christian IV it had experienced a wave of new culture and fine building. The "Great Builder," as he was known, had effectively doubled the size of the city during the earlier part of the century, building the Christianshavn area just across the harbour channel on Amager Island as an Amsterdam-like complex of narrow canals, homes, and warehouses, and going on to create a new housing district (Nyboder) to the northwest of Kongens Nytorv. His original yellow-wash rows of sailors' houses remain standing today. On a grander architectural scale, he was responsible for the existence of so many of the monumental green copper roofs that make the Copenhagen skyline uniquely photogenic in the 20th century—most notably among them the Round Tower, the Stock Exchange, and the magnificent Rosenborg Castle.

Absolute Power

As a result of the Swedish wars, Denmark was bankrupted and its country laid waste. Political and social upheaval were both inevitable.

In 1660, King Frederik III matched the mood of the moment and proclaimed himself absolute monarch, thereby depriving all the nobles of the Council of the Danish Realm of the powers they had enjoyed almost without a break since 1282. However, Frederik's absolute rule presided over a period of national unity, with a tightly controlled, well-organized central bureaucracy.

The early absolutist kings still waged several costly wars, mainly against the Swedish. Copenhagen suffered a terrible plague in 1711–1712 which killed off 22,000 people—nearly a third of its inhabitants—as well as two devastating fires in 1728 and 1795 which necessitated major reconstruction of much of the city.

Despite these setbacks, the 18th century was highlighted by major social advancements. Serfdom was abolished in 1788 (note the Freedom Pillar in Vesterbrogade, opposite the Central Station), and peasants threw off the yoke of the me-

The picturesque old town of Arthus, located on the Jutland peninsula.

dieval landlord and worked for themselves. They moved away from the central farmhouse, to construct their own dwellings and small-holdings in the surrounding fields. This self-emancipation gave the Danish countryside its present character of a landscape dotted with farms, and was of enormous influence in the shaping of modern Denmark.

Napoleon and the 19th Century

Denmark found itself reluctantly involved in the revolutionary wars of late-18th-century Europe. By maintaining their participation with Russia, Sweden, and Prussia in the League of Armed Neutrality—intended to thwart Great Britain's claim to the right of searching all vessels at sea—Denmark brought down upon itself the ire of the British. In 1801, a fleet under admirals Nelson and Parker sailed into the bay of Copenhagen. During the ensuing battle, Nelson, so legend has it, raised a telescope to his blind eye so as to be able to deny having been aware of a signal to break off the engagement.

Afraid that Napoleon would take over the Dano-Norwegian fleet, Britain subsequently demanded its instant surrender. When the Danes refused to accede, Copenhagen was blockaded and in 1807 subjected to a three-day bombardment by the British Navy. Denmark had no choice but to hand over what was left of its fleet to the British, only to be forced immediately afterwards to agree to an alliance with Napoleon, who was by then marching fast into Jutland.

When Napoleon was finally brought to his knees, Denmark emerged completely isolated on account of this alliance. Norway, already the home to a vigorous separatist movement, was handed over to Sweden in 1814 in payment of war debts, since Denmark's coffers had become empty. The formerly vast Danish territories overseas were reduced to Greenland, Iceland, the Faroes, and the Virgin Islands.

Fifty years later Denmark was to lose also the duchies of Schleswig and Holstein—a third of its home territory and two-fifths of its population—to Bismarck's Prussia. Following a spate of civil turmoil in Denmark provoked by the 1848 revolution in France, Frederik VII was forced to relinquish his absolute rule and hand over the reigns of power to the National Liberal Party.

A liberal constitution was drawn up with wide suffrage, and the Danish "Golden Age" was all set to begin. Søren Kierkegaard shook up contemporary philosophy and Christian religion with radical new proto-existentialist writings. Bertel Thorvaldsen, the great Danish sculptor, returned from Italy and left many monumental works in Copenhagen. Hans Christian Andersen was strolling the city streets, reading his fairy-tales to groups of admirers and rapidly becoming world-famous.

In the city, the old ramparts were demolished and new railroads, factories, and workers' housing blocks sprang up, so that by the late 19th century Copenhagen was a thriving industrial centre. In the last quarter of the century, social insurance schemes began to make an appearance—a bold and pioneering development.

Meanwhile, changes were beginning to take place in the countryside. N.F.S. Grundtvig, a leading European educationalist, had established his system of popular adult high schools in 1844 to improve the peasant's lot, and the first co-operative schemes were afoot.

The 20th Century

In 1901 an important landmark was reached in Danish constitutional history when a government based only on a majority in the lower chamber of parliament (*Folketing*) was appointed. The march of the common people brought them not only into the cities and urban areas, but also right into the political strug-

The Tivoli Boys Guard entertain both children and adults at Tivoli amusement park.

gle. In 1915, the Liberal Democrats, Social Democrats, and Radical Liberals jointly forced the abolition of electoral privileges in the upper chamber (*Landstinget*) and initiated a system of proportional representation for both chambers. At the same time, the vote was at last given to women and servants.

The new Danish society was put under severe strain in the process of adopting the compromises necessary to maintain neutrality during World War I. After the war North Schleswig voted itself back into Denmark, establishing the shape of today's border.

Industrial unrest and the severe economic depression between the two world wars failed to halt the progress of Denmark. In the sciences, theoretical physicist Niels Bohr of Copenhagen University was making fundamental contributions to atomic research. In architecture, Arne Jacobsen won a competition in 1929 for a circular, sun-rotating "house of the future" capable of accommodating an aircraft on the roof. Elsewhere, in the design of consumer goods—furniture, cutlery, glass, pewter, silver, and textiles—Denmark set new standards, combining utility with beauty, to the point where "Danish design" became synonymous with good, functional, yet aesthetically pleasing articles.

When World War II broke out in 1939, the Scandinavian countries issued declarations of neutrality, but on 9 April 1940 Denmark was invaded. Following a token struggle, the country's defences collapsed and the nation fell under German control. The Danish economy now found itself forced to adapt to the German market, and the country had no choice but to manifest a degree of compliance. However, the anti-Nazi sentiments of the vast majority of Danes were expressed by cold-shoulder treatment, and eventually acted upon through outright resistance. The Danes managed by various means to smuggle 7,000 of Denmark's 7,500 Jews out of the country to neighbouring Sweden.

The wartime king, Christian X, became the country's folk-hero as he rode out every day among the crowds. In 1943, the government resigned—it could no longer yield to German demands without losing the support of the population—and the running of the country was left to heads of departments. Nevertheless, the resistance was so organized and so dominant that Denmark was already a full member of the Allied forces by the time the war came to an end in 1945.

So began a new era of massive Danish reconstruction, finally resulting in the present modern-day society—one of the world's most successful attempts at a "welfare state"—with a quality of life ranking certainly among the highest in the world.

Politically, Denmark abandoned neutrality when it became a member of NATO in 1949. Economically, it was a founder-member of the European Free Trade Association (EFTA), and transferred into the European Economic Community (subsequently the European Union) with the U.K. and Ireland in 1972. It also played a part in the revival of Nordic unity after the war, joining the Nordic Council and the Nordic Council of Ministers.

Denmark today is one of the most prosperous countries in Europe, and its population of 5 million enjoys an extremely high standard of living. Membership to the European exchange rate mechanism has ensured that its economy continues to grow in strength. The country made its biggest impact to date on the European Union in a 1992 referendum, when over 50 percent of the population voted against the Maastricht Treaty (which lays the foundation for European economic and political union). At the World Summit in Copenhagen in 1995, Dennmark was one of the only countries to forgive a sizeable amount of Third-World debt. Denmark gained greater notoriety with the selection of Copenhagen as the 1996 "Cultural Capital of Europe." The fact that Denmark's influence is felt so far beyond its frontiers testifies to its important role in the future of a cohesive and integrated Europe.

Rosenborg Slot holds a collection of Danish crown jewels and other relics.

WHERE TO GO

You should have no problem finding your way around the delightfully compact and eminently walkable city of Copenhagen. Most of the important sights are contained within the central section bounded by the former medieval ramparts, and the city's many pedestrianized areas make exploring on foot a real pleasure. Copenhagen's abundance of leafy parks and gardens provide a welcome retreat from shopping or sightseeing, while its network of canals offers ample scope for waterside walks and gentle excursions afloat.

RÅDHUSPLADSEN

Every city has a heart somewhere, and Copenhagen's is Rådhuspladsen (Town Hall Square), without a doubt. Most planned walks, like ours, begin from here, as do all the buses you will need for city tours and trips to surrounding countryside, castles, and beaches.

Stand with your back to the red-brick Town Hall (Rådhuset) on the vast paved area of the Town Hall Square, and observe Danish life pass by. Here also you'll find your first hot-dog stand (pølsevogn), where tasty Danish sausages are served in a variety of inexpensive forms. The unique Tivoli pleasure gardens (see page 46) are already visible over to your left, just beyond the eight-lane H.C. Andersens Boulevard, where you'll notice at once a very prominent feature of Danish life—the bicycle. At rush hours, there seems to be millions of them.

The capital's most famous pedestrians-only street starts just a few metres to your right. Strøget (pronounced stroy-et) winds its way along for 1 km (about ¾ mile) to another main square, Kongens Nytorv, changing name several times along the way and never officially called Strøget. Most of the surrounding area is pedestrians-only, too, and you can satisfy

Copenhagen Highlights

(See also Museum Highlights on page 54)

Amalienborg Palace. *Amalienborg Slotsplads:* Four elegant Rococo palaces have been home to the Danish Royal Family since the 1750s; the changing of the guard at noon is a joy to behold. The palace is closed to the public, but a museum in King Christian VIII's Palace gives a glimpse of late-19th-century royal life (see page 36).

Christiansborg Slot. *Christiansborg Slotsplads:* The castle constructed over Bishop Absalon's original 12th-century edifice houses a complex of museums as well as government ministries and the Danish Parliament (*Folketing*). *Royal Reception Chambers:* conducted tours June–August Tues–Sun 11am, 1pm, and 3pm, September–May Tues–Sun 11am and 3pm; 37kr adults, 10kr children, free with Copenhagen Card (see page 53).

Den Lille Havfrue. *Langelinie:* Edvard Eriksen's bronze sculpture of Andersen's forlorn Little Mermaid gazing wistfully out to sea is Copenhagen's most famous statue (see page 39).

Rosenborg Slot. *Øster Voldgade 4A:* Christian IV's elegant Dutch Renaissance palace is a dazzling showcase for exhibits spanning 500 years of Danish royal history; highlights include the crown jewels and magnificent Long Hall. April–May and September–last week in October daily 11am–3pm, June–August daily 10am–4pm; 45kr adults, 10kr children, free with Copenhagen Card (see page 62).

Rundetårn. *Købmagergade:* The astronomical observatory built by Christian IV in 1642 is one of Copenhagen's distinctive landmarks; access to the top of the tower is by a unique 209-metre- (687-foot-) tall spiral causeway. *Tower:* September, April, and May daily 10am–5pm, June–August daily 10am–8pm. *Observatory:* October–March Tues–Wed 7–10pm; 15kr adults, 5kr children (see page 44).

Tivoli. *Vesterbrogade 3:* Opened in 1843, this old-time pleasure park in the heart of the city still draws the crowds. Daily end-April–mid-September; 39kr adults, 20kr children (see page 46).

most of your shopping needs with hardly a motorized vehicle in sight.

In the vast open square of Rådhuspladsen the statues leap to your attention—only a hint of the many hundreds scattered throughout the town. On the west corner of the square is the dramatic **Bull-and-Dragon Fountain** (1923), in copper, depicting a fierce, watery battle between the two beasts. Not far away sits a bronze version of Denmark's favourite son, storyteller Hans Christian Andersen, brooding by the boulevard that bears his name. Glance left down Vesterbrogade for a third statue: dividing the highway near to the Central Station is the Freedom Pillar, erected between 1792 and 1797 to commemorate the end of serfdom for the Danish peasantry in 1788.

Next, to your right on Vester Voldgade, is a statue that brings a smile to every Dane's face—the **Lur Blowers Stat-**

ue. Local legend has it that the two ancient men on top will sound a note on their instruments if a virgin passes by; though standing on the column since 1914, they've led a life of silence.

The **Town Hall** was built between 1892 and 1905. Its main doorway is crowned by a statue of Bishop Absalon, the founder of the city (see page 12), in copper and 22-carat gilt. If you then direct

Famed storyteller Hans Christian Andersen is memorialzed in bronze.

your view to the roof above you'll see the rest of our intro-
ductory statues—six bronze figures of nightwatchmen dating
from various periods of the city's history.

Each section of the Town Hall bears a different style and
imprint, but they come together architecturally in the same
way as a patchwork quilt. The main hall and the banqueting
room are impressive with their statuary and coats-of-arms—
especially the view of the 44-metre- (145-foot-) long hall
from the first-floor colonnade.

There is only one way to see the Town Hall, and that is by
guided tour. The two standard tours both leave from the entrance hall—each hour for the main tour and each half-hour
for Jens Olsen's **World Clock.** Consult the lists here for the
current schedules.

If it's a windy day, you'll be feeling a fresh breeze from
the Baltic beyond the harbour. The Town Hall stands on the
ancient shore-line; the waves would have been lapping at
your feet in days gone by.

We have divided the sights into four convenient tours, designed for walking. Turn to the the map on the inside cover
of this guide for easy reference.

THE OLD TOWN AND STRØGET

This first walk takes in some of the major sights, and the
pedestrianized Strøget area.

Crossing at the lights between Vester Voldgade and Rådhuspladsen, turn towards the Lur Blowers Statue and into the
first narrow street on your left, Lavendelstræde. Here you
will find typical Danish houses and shops from 1796, the
year following the city's second great fire, as well as a view
ahead of the massive masonry and archways of Copenhagen's fourth town hall. Built between 1805 and 1815, it
now houses the country's principal law courts.

The Strøget changes names four times in its three-quarter-mile length, but it always stays car-free.

On the right as you turn into Hestemøllestræde is a corner house where Mozart's widow lived with her second husband, a Danish diplomat. Carry on across the next junction into Gåsegade, and look out for the gabled houses with 18th-century hoists at the top—furniture is traditionally hauled up by hoists, rather than being squeezed up narrow stairwells.

At the end of Gåsegade, on the left hand side, is a delightful little **square,** a suntrap on good days, with a pretty fountain. The name of the square, Vandkunsten, means "water artifice," and here Copenhagen's first water pipes were laid.

Cross into Magstræde and go back in time. At numbers 17 and 19 are two of the city's oldest houses, dating from 1640. Opposite is the excellent youth centre, **Huset** ("the house"). Besides having a jazz club and cinema, folk club, theatre, and bars, Huset offers a wealth of advice, information, and brochures for young travellers, including how to keep out of trouble—or deal with it if you're in it. The entrance is at Rådhusstræde 13.

Continue straight on, past interesting courtyards, Snaregade, and finally some timber-framed houses, into **Gammel Strand** (meaning "old shore"). As its name implies, this is the former edge of the city, and over the present-day canal you get your first glimpse of magnificent, green-roofed Christiansborg—now the home of parliament, but once a royal palace—built on an island.

Gammel Strand is a place to pause and prime your camera; it's a fine old waterfront. To the far right on Frederiksholms Kanal you'll be able to make out the arched entrance to the colossal **Nationalmuseet** (see page 60). Immediately across the canal lies the distinctive sight of a square-arched, yellow-ochre building with a decorated Classical-style frieze, looking like a national tomb. That's really what it is—a

Rådhusplasen, Copenhagen's Town Hall Square, is the centre and the heart of the city.

Christiansborg Slot is the sixth palace to be built on this site in the last 800 years.

monument to the great Danish sculptor Bertel Thorvaldsen (1770–1844). Built between 1839 and 1848, **Thorvaldsens Museum** contains a mass of statuary, and the frieze depicts the sculptor's triumphant return from Rome in 1838.

Gammel Strand is one of the two principal starting-points for canal boat tours, the other being in Nyhavn (see page 34).

A few yards farther along, near Højbro Plads, stands the **statue of the Fiskerkone** (Fishwife), scarf on her head, wraps around her shoulders, wearing a stout apron and clasping a fish. Erected in 1940, she resembles the women who sit inside their stalls nearby every Tuesday to Friday morning, as fishwives have here for centuries.

In the near distance rears the magnificent **statue of Bishop Absalon.** Copper-green, displaying the warrior-priest in chainmail with axe in hand, the statue makes a most impressive picture against the background of red-tiled gable roofs and the soaring copper steeple of Skt Nikolaj Kirke (St. Nicholas Church), now an art gallery, café, and exhibition centre.

As you cross over Højbro to Christiansborg Slotsplads, the square fronting onto the main entrance for the **Christiansborg complex,** look to your left over the bridge. The unusual sculpture you'll be able to see below the water is "Mermaid with Seven Sons," attractively illuminated at night.

Christiansborg is the sixth castle or palace to have stood here since Absalon built his fortress in 1167—pillage, fire, and rebuilding frenzies having taken their toll. The third castle became the permanent seat of the king and government in 1417. The present edifice dates from the beginning of the 20th century, when an architectural competition for the design of a new Christiansborg was won by Thorvald Jørgensen. On 15 November 1907, King Frederik VIII laid the foundation-stone hewn out of the granite remains from Absalon's castle. Above this a vast plinth was made of about 7,500 boulders donated by 750 Danish boroughs, and then the palace was faced with granite slabs. Look up to see 57 granite masks of Denmark's greatest men. Covered in copper in 1937–1939, the roof of Christiansborg makes an imposing addition to the city's typical green skyline.

The chapel, theatre museum, riding lodges, and beautifully restored **marble bridge,** which managed to survive two disastrous fires in 1794 and 1884, help to give the palace a more venerable aspect than its mainly recent origins suggest.

The palace's interior holds enough delights to fill a whole day—see page 53 for further details—but for the moment we'll continue along the canal as far as the highly ornamented **Børsen** (Stock Exchange), dating from the days of Christian IV. Its green copper roof is topped by a famous spire composed of four twining dragon's tails. Christian IV was influenced by the booming Netherlands architecture of his day, and in 1619 commissioned two Dutch brothers to put up this somewhat quaint building. This building currently houses special events. The Stock Exchange has since emigrated to Strøget.

Glance to your left over the canal, past the Børsgade street flower market, and see another building rising straight out of the water, Venetian-style but with Dutch gable ends and a small copper tower in the middle. The building was originally a 16th-century anchor forge. However, in 1619 Christian IV transformed it into a sailors' church. **Holmens Kirke** (open Monday thorough Saturday 9:00 A.M. to noon) is a real surprise when you walk inside: it's small and cosy, giving an impression of warmth and wood. On the altar, the reredos, and the pulpit, there's a veritable outburst of oak carving by Abel Schrøder the Younger, who became famous through these works.

Holmens Kirke remains a favourite with the Royal Family; in 1967 Queen Margrethe was married in the church to Prince Henrik, formerly the French Count de Laborde de Montpezat. It holds a special place in the affections of naval men, also, as an adjoining chapel (added in 1706–1708) is dedicated to sea heroes, from the 17th-century admiral Baron Niels Juel to Danish sailors who died in World War II. Two ship models hang from the ceiling of the church, a deep-seated tradition you'll note in many other Danish churches.

Up Admiralgade opposite the church, on the other side of the Holmens Kanal street, you approach the 70-metre- (230-foot-) tall spire of Skt Nikolaj Kirke, which will have come into view regularly since the fishwives' corner. Destroyed several times by fire, it was rebuilt as recently as 1917. It is no longer used for services, only for public events such as art exhibitions.

Walk along Vingårdsstræde and you'll find yourself in an area of jazz clubs, small bars, and artists' dives; go over Bremerholm, on to Kongens Nytorv (see page 32), then left into the northeast end of **Strøget.**

Strøget is a charming and delightful traffic-free urban island to stroll along, by day or in the evening, with its numerous small bars, cafés, and excellent shops. It changes name four times during its three-quarter-mile course. At the Kon-

Copenhagen, as seen from above: both a modern and an ancient city.

gens Nytorv end, it begins as Østergade, then turns into Amagertorv, Vimmelskaftet, Nygade, and Frederiksberggade.

Along the first stretch, off Østergade to the right, **Pistolstræde** is a picturesque alley lined with restaurants and shops from five centuries of Copenhagen history. Return to Strøget and farther on, at Amagertorv 6, you'll see a fine example of Dutch Baroque, the Royal Copenhagen porcelain showroom. Shortly after is the 17th- to 18th-century **Helligåndskirke** (Church of the Holy Ghost), with its grassy square.

Continue along Strøget. As you pass by Hyskenstræde and Badstuestræde, you're in an area of side-streets well worth investigating further if you're interested in antiques, curios, and unusual little shops.

Strøget now opens out into a broad pedestrian area comprising the two squares of Gammeltorv and Nytorv and a cluster of

Look for the red box with the crown and bugle if you've got postcards to send.

pavement cafés. On Nytorv you have a full-frontal view of the simple yet powerful law courts. The **Caritas Fountain** on Gammeltorv is the city's oldest, dating from 1610. It is traditional (dating from the golden wedding of King Christian IX and Queen Louise in 1892) to make imitation golden apples dance on the jets on the monarch's birthday (now 16 April).

Strøget finally changes into Frederiksberggade, and 180 metres (200 yards) away lies our starting point, Rådhuspladsen.

KONGENS NYTORV AND THE HARBOUR

This walk begins at **Kongens Nytorv** (buses 1, 6, 28, 29, and 41 from Rådhuspladsen), the "king's new square" of Christian V, dating from 1680 and still the city's largest square, with 12 streets leading off of it.

Setting the tone for the 3 hectares (8 acres) of Kongens Nytorv is **Det kongelige Teater** (Danish Royal Theatre), situated on the southwest side. This theatre, the country's most important cultural centre, is the home of Danish national ballet, opera, and drama. Originally opened in 1748, rebuilt in 1874, it was briefly the stage of Hans Christian Andersen, who tried without success to become a ballet dancer here.

The house one door along, fronting the south side of Nyhavn canal, is said to be the most important work of pure Baroque remaining today in Denmark. Called **Charlotten-**

borg because Queen Charlotte Amalie lived here from 1700, it has functioned since 1754 as the seat of the Royal Danish Academy of Art.

Erected between 1672 and 1683 by the illegitimate son of King Frederik III, Ulrik Frederik Gyldenløve, Charlottenborg was of great architectural importance in Denmark. Not only were many country mansions modelled after this redbrick Dutch Baroque design by a Dutch architect, Evert Janssen, but Ulrik also made the nobility build alongside him in Kongens Nytorv and develop the square in a manner worthy of its royal name.

Consequently, if you look around you'll notice a number of other fine buildings: **Thotts Palæ** (Thott's Mansion) in the northeast corner, built for the naval hero Admiral Niels Juel

The Danish Royal Theatre's stage was once the stomping ground of Hans Christian Andersen.

To the right, Nyhavn, or New Harbour; above, a tour boat gliding down the oft-photographed City Canal.

and now the French Embassy; and the quaint triangular building that stands between Store Strandstræde and Bredgade, the beautifully preserved 1782 **Kanneworffs Hus.**

Centrepiece of the square is an elaborate equestrian statue of Christian V, with four Classical figures seated submissively under his horse.

Now walk across the square towards **Nyhavn.** The name literally means "new harbour"; you'll immediately notice the nautical flavour of this one-time "sailors' street." At this end of the canal, dug into the middle of the city in 1671 to enlarge the harbour facilities, stands a sizeable old anchor, a memorial to the Danish sailors killed in World War II.

Over the centuries the two sides of this canal have developed into a unique illustration of old Copenhagen. Much painted and photographed, Nyhavn is today a mix of boutiques, antiques stores, taverns, and restaurants on its immediate north side, and elsewhere a collection of elegantly restored frontages, luxury apartments, some good restaurants, and one superb hotel conversion of an 18th-century warehouse.

For two periods of his life Hans Christian Andersen lived in Nyhavn, first at number 67 from 1854 to 1864 and later at number 18. This is a street with everything—history, architecture, nightlife, a constant passage of colourful small boats,

The changing of the guard at Amalienborg is a daily event fraught with ceremony.

and also a terminus for canal-boat tours as well as the hydrofoil service to Sweden.

Walk down Nyhavn (staying on the north side) until you come across a fine view looking out over the inner harbour to the Christianshavn area and the spiralling steeple of Vor Frelsers Kirke (see page 48).

Bear round left to Skt Annæ Plads, a boulevard lined with consulates and fine old offices, then right into Amaliegade and through a wooden colonnaded archway into the stately square of **Amalienborg Palace.** All things here are in studied symmetry. On four of the eight sides stand identical mansion-like palaces. From each one juts two wings. Four roads then converge at right angles on the courtyard, while 16 bearskin-topped soldiers guard each of the palaces and corners, with an extra sentry posted at the gateway. The queen lives in the right-hand wing next to the colonnade, the queen mother lives in the adjacent wing, and the two princes live in the third, which houses in addition the Amalienborg Palace museum (see page 54). The fourth, directly to the left, is reserved as a guest house for state visitors.

Amalienborg was given its name after the wife of Frederik III, Queen Sophie Amalie, but the buildings burned down in 1689. The present mansions on the same site were originally designed as noblemen's homes by the court architect Nicolai Eigtved during a city expansion in the 1750s. After Christiansborg castle was destroyed by fire for a second time in 1794, the royal family slowly bought up Amalienborg from the nobles, and has lived here since. Today the palace is reckoned to be one of the finest Rococo ensembles in Europe. Its centre-piece is a copper **equestrian monument** to King Frederik V.

The main Amalienborg attraction is the **changing of the guard.** At 11:30 each morning, when the queen is in residence, the guards leave their barracks near Rosenborg Castle and march through the city back streets so as to arrive in the palace square just before noon, moving from one sentry-box to another in a series of foot-stamping ceremonies. Up to 70 guardsmen march in accompanied by a full band, black bearskins rippling in the breeze, wearing white-

The Gefion Fountain, depicting the Nordic goddess and her four "sons."

striped blue trousers and highly polished boots, and, on festive occasions, red tunics with white shoulder straps.

The popular **Amaliehaven** gardens lie between Amalienborg Palace and the harbour. They were created by Belgian landscape architect Jean Delogne using French limestone and Danish granite, while the bronze pillars around the fountain were designed by Italian sculptor Arnaldo Pomodoro.

Keep strolling north along Amaliegade again to the junction with Esplanaden, where several sights come into view.

Frihedsmuseet (the Danish Resistance Movement Museum; see also page 59), located on one of the prettiest spots in town (especially at daffodil time), also offers the opportunity for a lunchtime snack at the cafeteria.

One of Copenhagen's most recognizable icons: the Little Mermaid, caught between water and land at Langelinie.

St. Alban's Church resembles a typical English country church, and was indeed constructed by an English architect amid the green lawns of Churchill Park in 1887.

A spectacle that will arrest your attention even longer is the **Gefion Fountain,** Copenhagen's most spectacular, put up by the Carlsberg Foundation in 1908, depicting the legend of the Nordic goddess Gefion, who turned her four sons into oxen and used them to plough the island of Zealand out of Sweden. Sculptor Anders Bundgaard's monument makes dramatic use of a small slope near the church, so that as the goddess and her "sons" drive down it, a massive spray of water flies up around.

Follow the right-hand path behind the fountain to Langelinie through delightful gardens, until you arrive at the most famous statue of all, the **Little Mermaid** (*Den Lille Havfrue*). In Andersen's fairy-tale, this tragic sea-girl exchanged her voice for human legs in order to gain the love

of an earthly prince, but mutely had to watch as he jilted her for a real princess. In desperation, she threw herself into the sea and turned to foam.

To the dismay of both visitors and Danes, the mermaid has frequently been vandalized. Recently her head was sawn off; another time she lost her arm. Luckily, the workshop of sculptor Edvard Eriksen retains the original moulds from 1913, and new parts can be cast if necessary.

You can continue half a mile to **Langelinie** itself—a colourful quay when the tour ships are in—or take a detour into the Citadel gardens nearby.

Kastellet (the Citadel) was a cornerstone of Christian IV's defences of Copenhagen. The 300-year-old fort (most of it built between 1662 and 1725) is still in use by the army, and the church, prison, and main guardhouse have resisted the assaults of time. It is a delightfully peaceful enclave, with a charming windmill (1847) and some remains of the old ramparts well worth seeing.

Within walking distance of the Citadel is **Nyboder** ("new dwellings"), erected between 1631 and 1641 by King Christian IV for his sailors. Painted yellow, with steep gable roofs and shuttered windows, they form a fashionable, well-preserved community of houses still inhabited by navy personnel, set in the triangle where Øster Voldgade meets Store Kongensgade.

Leave the Citadel garden by way of the southern exit onto Esplanaden, and turn towards **Bredgade.** The area between here and Kongens Nytorv is a residential quarter of substantial granite houses and quadrangles, once very fashionable, planned by architect Nicolai Eigtved at about the same time as Amalienborg. At number 70 there is a plaque commemorating the death of philosopher Søren Kierkegaard in 1855. At number 68 you'll find the **Kunstindustrimuseet** (Museum of Decorative Art), a fine Rococo building and former 18th-century hospital (see page 59).

Almost next door, at number 64, is Skt Ansgar Kirke, centre of the modest Roman Catholic community since 1842. A museum documents the history of Catholicism in the city since its virtual extinction in the Reformation of 1536.

Before two stately mansions on the corner of Fredericiagade appear the golden onion-shaped domes of **Alexander**

Newsky Kirke, built for the Russian Orthodox community between 1881 and 1883.

As Bredgade opens out at the junction with Frederiksgade, the great dome of **Marmorkirken** (Marble Church) rises high to your right. Measuring 31 metres (100 feet) in diameter, this is one of the largest church domes in Europe. First planned around 1740 by Nicolai Eigtved as the centre-point of this new "Frederik's Town" area (the church is also known as *Frederikskirken*), its foundation stone was laid by King Frederik V in 1749. However, by 1770 the Norwegian marble required for the building had become so expensive that the project was called to a halt, and it remained standing for a century as a picturesque ruin. It was eventually consecrated in 1894, the Norwegian marble having been complemented by Danish marble from Faxe.

The Marmorkirken was completed with the addition of some Danish marble.

Inside, it's both impressive and beautiful. The dome, carried on 12 stout pillars, is decorated with rich frescoes in blue, gold, and green. Outside, the church is surrounded by statues of personalities of the Danish Church, ranging from St. Ansgar (who helped bring the Christian religion to Denmark) to Grundtvig, the 19th-century educationalist. On the

roof are 16 figures from religious history, from Moses to Luther.

This is an excellent place to rest before concluding your walk down Bredgade.

UNIVERSITY QUARTER AND PARKS

From Rådhuspladsen, this time go west for a short way along Vester Voldgade and then turn right into narrow Studiestræde, the home to a motley collection of antiques shops, bookstalls, and boutiques gathered in an 18th-century setting.

At number 6 Studiestræde a plaque records that H.C. Ørsted, discoverer of electro-magnetism in 1820, lived here. A few yards farther on, at the corner of Nørregade, you will

The Chinese Tower, just one of many diverse attractions at Tivoli pleasure park.

come across one of Copenhagen's oldest preserved buildings, the former **Bispegården** (Bishop's Residence), built in 1500 and now part of the university. Nearby on Bispetorvet stands a monument erected in 1943 commemorating the 400th anniversary of the introduction of the Reformation to Denmark. Over the square looms the sombre shape of the Cathedral (*Domkirken*) of Copenhagen,

known as **Vor Frue Kirke** (Church of Our Lady). Bishop
Absalon's successor, Sunesen, is said to have laid its foundations in the 12th century, but by 1316 it had already
burned down four times. Later, two further constructions
were destroyed—by the great 1728 fire and by British
bombardment in 1807. The present church was reconstructed by V.F.K. and C.F. Hansen in 1811–1829. Its large austere interior is relieved by a collection of heroic statues by
Bertel Thorvaldsen; twelve massive marble Apostles line
the aisle, while an orange-lit altar is surrounded with
bronze candelabra and dominated by the famous **figure of
Christ** by Thorvaldsen.

The main university block to the north of the cathedral
dates back in its present form only as far as the 1830s, but
Copenhagen University itself was founded in 1479. This is a
typical student area, with sidewalk cafés and a number of
fascinating bookshops.

Behind the cathedral and the university runs Fiolstræde, a delightful pedestrians-only street. Just down
Krystalgade stands the Synagogue of Copenhagen, inaugurated in 1833.

Retrace your path down Fiolstræde, and make the detour
into Skindergade, where you'll find **Gråbrødretorv**—a picturesque square surrounded by brightly painted 18th-century
houses which was the site of a Franciscan monastery until
the Reformation. Cafés have proliferated here in recent
years; it's a good place for a break.

Making your way in the direction of Købmagergade, first by
Lille Kannikestæde, then going right along Store Kan-
nikestræde, glance into the exquisite courtyard at number 10 if
the gates are open. Admiral Ove Gjedde constructed this tim-
bered mansion in 1637, echoing King Christian IV's wish that
Copenhagen's beauty should be a joy forever.

The pleasant street of **Købmagergade** is one of Copenhagen's oldest commercial thoroughfares. Here the ubiquitous builder Christian IV laid the foundation stone of **Trinitatis Kirke** (Trinity Church) in 1637 and built the **Rundetårn** (Round Tower) in 1642 as an astronomical observatory. The Round Tower has been one of the city's most beloved landmarks for 300 years, even if it only reaches the modest height of 35 metres (115 feet). It is more interesting to visit than the rather conventional church. You can walk to the top, but not by any ordinary means—steps would have been impractical for

raising the heavy equipment needed here. Instead, a wide spiral causeway winds its way round for 209 metres (687 feet) inside the tower. Not only did Czar Peter the Great ride up to the top on horseback in 1716, but his empress followed him in a coach-and-six.

Students have been living in the Regensen university hostel, opposite the Round Tower, since 1623. Most of the building standing today is 18th-century, with the notable addition of an arcade built in 1909.

One art attraction certainly worth a visit while in this area is the **Musikhistorisk Museum** (Musical History Museum)

The bright colours of the Pantomime Theatre at Tivoli are the backdrop for some very energetic entertainment.

at Åbenrå 30, which holds a fine collection of old instruments and musical literature. Be sure not to forget **Davids Samling** (David's Art Collection), which is located at Kronprinsessegade 30 (see page 57).

The street beside the Round Tower that is signposted "Landemærket" leads on to the main road, Gothersgade, and a wide expanse of parkland and some botanical gardens, as well as one of the most appealing castles to be found in any city.

Tivoli

Tivoli is magic, something you can't explain by statistics, its ambience created by both chance and inspiration. It's a reflection of the Danes' desire to enjoy themselves in pleasurable surroundings, a place for all the family and all generations to be together and have fun.

In the heart of the city and on the site of ancient fortifications, Tivoli is uniquely placed as a pleasure park. Here, you'll find two different worlds by day and by night. You can stay from 10am to midnight on one ticket (cheaper than cinema).

400,000 flowers are blooming at any one time, trees and pathways are lit by 110,000 electric light bulbs (no neon here), there are free fireworks shows three nights a week, and myriad snack bars, restaurants, cafés, and beer houses serve anything from hot-dogs to gourmet meals. (You can bring *smørrebrød* from the Vesterbrogade shops to a restaurant by the lake, buy coffee, and freely use plates, cutlery, and napkins.)

There's a Chinese pagoda restaurant beside an arcade of lively slot machines; a concert hall offering everything from the Berlin Philharmonic to the Århus Fire Brigade Band; some 85 shops; merry-go-rounds for the kids; a pantomime theatre; coloured fountains by the lake; and a Tivoli Boy Guard's Band marching through like the Queen's Life Guard in miniature.

Five million people visit it each year, equivalent to the entire population of Denmark. Some 300 million have paid to gain admission since Georg Carstensen was granted a royal licence for the site in 1843. The 8-hectare (20-acre) pleasure park, the size of nine city blocks, is privately operated, on lease from Copenhagen Council.

Open from the end of April to mid-September, Tivoli produces its own programme of events, available on the spot.

Directly opposite the end of Landemærket is the **Kongens Have** park, laid out in 1606–1607 when Christian IV announced that Christiansborg Palace was becoming too official and oppressive. At the same time, he began to build a small country mansion for himself in a corner of the site (it was then situated beyond the town walls), which he eventually expanded into **Rosenborg Slot** (Castle), since 1833 a royal museum of considerable grace and character (see page 62). Christian helped to plan this three-storey brick building in Dutch-Danish Renaissance style. It is as cosy a a castle as you'll ever find. It has all the frills and furbelows, turrets and towers, moats and battlemented gateways characteristic of a "proper" castle, yet retains the atmosphere of a weekend retreat.

Gardeners will be interested in the **Botanisk Have** (Botanical Gardens) opposite Rosenborg, while art lovers should allow themselves time to explore the **Statens Museum for Kunst** (National Gallery) farther north up Øster Voldgade (see page 63.)

From here, bus 10 will take you to Kongens Nytorv, while 75E (rush hours) will transport you back to Rådhuspladsen.

CHRISTIANSHAVN

Though there's so much to see within a small radius of Rådhuspladsen and Kongens Nytorv, it's worth spending a few hours just the other side of the harbour channel, crossing over bridges Langebro or Knippelsbro into **Christianshavn,** and if time permits continuing on to the Amager villages of Store Magleby and Dragør.

The name Christianshavn, meaning Christian's Harbour, is derived from King Christian IV (once again); the whole area looks very much like a slice of Amsterdam, reflecting the king's predilection for Netherlands architecture.

Take bus 2 or 8 from Rådhuspladsen to Christianshavns Torv, then cross the main road and walk up **Overgaden oven Vandet** to see the Dutch-style warehouses, narrow houses, and small bars all topped by hoists, and a scene of multi-coloured boats on the canal.

Turn the corner to the right into Skt Annæ Gade, and a Danish-Italian sight will meet you—**Vor Frelsers Kirke** (Our Saviour's Church). This brick-and-sandstone church was built between 1682 and 1696 under the direction of Lambert van Haven. The distinctive spire, with a staircase spiralling outside the structure, was added more than half a century later by Lauridz de Thurah, said to have been influenced at the time by Sant'Ivo alla Sapienza church in Rome. A total of 400 steps (a third of them on the outside) lead from the entrance of the church to the gilt globe and Christ figure up on top of the spire, though you'll be allowed the rare experience of this outdoor climb—if you venture to take it—only in good weather.

A popular myth is that de Thurah made a mistake by designing the spiral the wrong way round, and on realizing this suddenly threw himself from the top. The spire was completed in 1752, however, and all the records indicate that he lived on another seven years.

The inside of the church is of interest not simply because of the choir screen guarded by six wooden angels, nor because of the ornate white marble font, supported by four cherubs, nor even because of the altar dating from 1732, and replete with allegorical statues and Dresden-like figures playing in the clouds. All this is crowned by the monumental organ, built in 1690 and several times remodelled, on the last occasion in 1965. Beautifully ornamented, the whole construction is supported by two large stucco elephants.

Elephants are something of a recurring theme in Denmark, perhaps traceable to the country's oldest order of chivalry, the Order of the Elephant. The central vault of the church is decorated with a monogram of Christian V, together with the royal coat-of-arms and a chain of the Order of the Elephant.

Our Saviour's is open Monday to Saturday from 9:00 A.M. to 3:30 P.M. (10:00 A.M. to 2:00 P.M. in winter) and from 11:30 A.M. to 1:30 P.M. on Sunday. You have to pay a small charge to climb the tower for the view of the city — though the tower is often undergoing repairs to keep it in condition.

Now retrace your path again along Skt Annæ Gade, and cross over the bridge to-

Heavenly steps wind their way up the length of the spire at Vor Frelsers Kirke.

wards the junction with **Strandgade,** opposite the Foreign Ministry. This area is a curious mixture of old and new. The Danish Centre for Architecture is a good example, a former warehouse at Gammel Dok. Turning left into the street of 17th- and 18th-century houses, take a peep into the cobbled courtyards, flanked by their numerous small living annexes. N.F.S. Grundtvig spent some years at number 4B. At number 6, in the early 18th century, lived Admiral Peter Wessel Tordenskjold—

Street artists at Town Hall Square on Amager Island.

a Dano-Norwegian hero who won battles at sea but whose exuberant lifestyle ashore lost him many good neighbours. It's said that every time he called *skål* during his frequent banquets, a salute would be fired from two cannons at the main doorway, with many a sleepless night had by all until his death in a duel in 1720.

Across the Torvegade, blocking off the end of Strandgade, lies the sombre **Christians Kirke.** Built in 1755 by Nicolai Eigtved, it possesses an unexpected interior layout, with arched galleries reminiscent of an old-time music-hall.

Next, the nearby Knippelsbro will bring you back towards the centre of the city, or there's an option to see some of Amager island and a quaint village by the sea.

OUTLYING SIGHTS

Public transport takes you out to suburban Copenhagen. To go south to the municipalities of Amager island, catch a 31 bus at Christianshavns Torv, and after about 1½ km (1 mile) change either to a 30 at Amager Boulevard or to a 33 at Sundholmsvej. You then drive through a large housing district and leave the airport route behind you (passing under the main runway) to reach the village of **Store Magleby,** untouched by time—except for the noise from the airport.

Here in an old farmhouse on the village street you'll find **Amagermuseet** (the Amager Museum), all laid out in old style, complete with furniture, bedrooms, and kitchen. Begun in 1901, the collection was donated by villagers from the surrounding area. In a straightforward manner the museum explains the reasons for the Dutch atmosphere that prevails over this area.

The Dutch connection first began when King Christian II (reigned 1513–1523) invited a colony of Netherlands farmers to come and improve soil cultivation in the area, and so provide the royal table with "as many roots and onions as are needed." He gave the Dutch special privileges to live in Store Magleby, which for centuries was referred to as Hollænder-byen (Dutchmen's Town). They had their own judicial system and church (with services in Dutch or Low German only), and developed a bizarre local costume—derived from Dutch, Danish, and French styles—a large collection of which is on display at the museum.

The Amager Museum stays open May through September Tuesday–Sunday noon to 4:00 P.M.; from October through April it is open only Wednesday and Sunday.

Hop aboard the 30 or 33 bus again for another 2½ km (1½ miles) to the water's edge at **Dragør,** where the harbour is packed with small boats and the 18th-century village remains remarkably preserved. A maze of cobbled streets and alleyways leads off from the only traffic road. You can walk around between yellow-wash buildings and postage-stamp gardens to get a vivid impression of what life was like before the internal combustion engine.

Beside the harbour a 1682 fisherman's cottage (the oldest house in the town) has been imaginatively converted into the **Dragør Museum,** devoted to local seafaring history. The museum is open May through September Tuesday–Friday 2:00 to 5:00 P.M., Saturday and Sunday noon to 6:00 P.M. From here, you can catch a 30 or 33 bus to make your way back to Rådhuspladsen.

Town Hall Square now provides the starting point for a trip to **Grundtvig's Memorial Church** in northwest Copenhagen at Bispebjerg. Here, a mere 10-minute journey from the centre (buses 16 and 19 from Rådhuspladsen), a total of six million bricks have been laid as a monument honouring the man who was once called Denmark's greatest son.

Founder of the Danish residential high schools, Nikolai Frederik Severin Grundtvig (1783–1872) was a renowned educationalist, austere parson, and prolific hymn-writer. Grundtvigs Kirke, built in his memory, is also a monument to early 20th-century Danish architecture. The church's design, by Peder Jensen-Klint, is extraordinarily simple but effective. A few chosen masons, some of them employed from start to finish, carried through the project between 1921 and 1940. Everything is in pale-yellow brick — the 49-metre- (160-foot-) tall tower and the vaults of the 22-metre (72-foot) nave, all the stairs and pillars, the balustrades, altar, and the pulpit.

Stainless-steel organ pipes (4,800 of them) look down on a vast, uncluttered nave. It's a fitting tribute to a man who composed 1,400 hymns, and a national monument that you should try not to miss.

Visiting hours are from mid-May to mid-September Monday–Saturday 9:00 A.M. to 4:45 P.M., Sunday noon to 4:00 P.M.; for the rest of the year hours are 9:00 A.M. to 4:00 P.M. during the week and noon to 1:00 P.M. on Sunday and holidays.

MUSEUMS

Hours may be subject to rapid change, and there's little consistency in admission charges. Some museums are free, many cost only a few kroner, while others charge a lot. Reductions for children are always available, varying between 50 and 80 percent; sometimes they even get in free. A worthwhile investment is the Copenhagen Card (see page 128), valid for up to three days, which offers free entry to a large number of the major museums. To avoid disappointments, be sure to check up on opening hours and bus routes before setting out.

Christiansborg Slot (Christiansborg Castle)

Today the castle houses government ministries, Parliament (*Folketing*), and also the Danish Supreme Court, as well as being the centre of a complex of museums.

The peaceful stretches of rolling countryside on the outskirts of Copenhagen are a pleasant contrast to the city.

Museum Highlights

Amalienborg Palace Museum: *Christian VIII's Palace, Amalienborg.* See for yourself how the Danish Royal Family lived between 1863 and 1947. Open May 11am to 4pm, January through April 11am to 4pm; 35kr adults, 5kr children, free with Copenhagen Card (see page 36).

Den Hirschsprungske Samling: *Stockholmsgade 20.* A delightful museum set in parkland and devoted to 19th-century Danish art, notably Golden Age painters. Open Wednesday 11am to 9pm, Thursday through Monday 11am to 4pm, closed Tuesday; 25kr adults, children free (see page 57).

Nationalmuseet: *Ny Vestergade 10.* The biggest museum in Scandinavia is a treasure trove of artefacts, from Stone Age rock carvings and Mongolian tents to Danish domestic interiors showing how people lived from the 17th century onwards. Open Tuesday through Sunday 10am to 5pm; 30kr adults, children free, also free with Copenhagen Card (see page 60).

Ny Carlsberg Glyptotek: *Dantes Plads 7.* The outstanding Classical collection of Danish brewer Carl Jacobsen is brought together under one elaborate roof; exhibitions of Egyptian, Greek, Roman, and Etruscan art feature alongside later works, including 73 bronze statuettes by Degas. Open Tuesday through Sunday 10am to 4pm; closed on Monday the whole year round; 15kr (see page 61).

Thorvaldsens Museum: *Porthusgade 2.* The works of the prolific Danish sculptor Bertel Thorvaldsen are housed in the city's most distinctive building. Open Tuesday through Sunday 10am to 5pm, guided tours in English Sunday 3pm; free (see page 63).

De Kongelige Repræsentationslokaler (Royal Reception Chambers). A fine starting point, but you must join a conducted tour. This is a no-touch museum with strict rules. One of the guide's first anecdotes is: "Look at the roof here, held by pillars in the shape of male statues, heads bent to take the weight—a symbol of modern Danes paying their taxes...." In the entrance-hall, canvas slippers are provided for you to put over your shoes, as you'll be walking on priceless parquet floors.

Upstairs is a series of linked rooms, including the richly tapestried gold-and-green room where monarchs are proclaimed from the balcony, which overlooks the Castle Square (*Slotspladsen*) below. (Danish monarchs have not actually been crowned since the day of Christian VIII, though a crowd of 50,000 attended the proclamation of the present Queen Margrethe II in 1972.)

In the palace basement, the extensive well-preserved brick and stone **ruins** of the previous palaces are worth a visit.

Royal Reception Chambers: conducted tours June through August Tuesday–Sunday 11:00 A.M., 1:00, and 3:00 P.M.; September and May Tuesday–Sunday 11:00 A.M., 3:00 P.M.; October through April Tuesday, Thursday, and Sunday 11:00 A.M. and 3:00 P.M. *Folketing:* tours every Sunday 10:00 to 11:00 A.M. and 1:00 to 4:00 P.M., also June through August daily except Saturday 10:00 A.M. to 4:00 P.M. *Palace ruins:* October through April Tuesday–Friday and Sunday, May through September daily, 9:30 A.M. to 3:30 P.M. (For the Royal Arsenal Museum, see page 56.)

Teatermuseet (Theatre Museum)

Chriastiansborg Ridebane 18; buses 1, 2, 5, 6, 8–10, 31, 37, and 43. Cross the royal riding grounds at the rear of Christiansborg—a scene dominated by a copper equestrian statue of Christian IX—and in an elegant terrace above the stables

The central hall of the Glyptotek Museum seems to be transplanted right from ancient Rome.

you'll discover an extraordinary theatre museum. The smell of horses seeps up through its 200-year-old creaky floorboards, and it has always been thus: at the Court Theatre's very first production in 1767, an authentic country odour was remarked.

The small auditorium and galleries are packed with Danish and international theatre relics—memorabilia of Ibsen, Anna Pavlova, and Hans Christian Andersen, as well as playbills, costumes, and photographs of Danish theatre history.

Open all year Wednesday 2:00 to 4:00 P.M., Saturday and Sunday noon to 4:00 P.M.

Tøjhusmuseet (Royal Arsenal Museum)

Tøj-husgade 3; buses 1, 2, 6, and 8 from Rådhuspladsen. Attendants wearing three-cornered hats and knee-length red jackets greet you in this vast building on the southeast side of

Christiansborg. It's appropriate for a museum housing one of Europe's most important collections of military uniforms and historic equipment.

In this museum everything is laid out open-plan, with very little set behind glass. Cannonballs are piled high like potato stacks. Guns on display range from a 15th-century cannon of the time of Queen Margrete I to sophisticated new weapons. Three old military planes from 1909, 1921, and 1925 are suspended from the roof, while upstairs is a glittering display of uniforms and small arms. Open Tuesday–Sunday noon to 4:00 P.M., closed Mondays.

Davids Samling (David's Art Collection)

Kronprinsessegade 30; buses 7, 10, and 43 from Kongens Nytorv. European fine arts from the 17th and 18th centuries; a variety of Persian medieval art, ceramics, and Danish 18th-century silverware. Open 1:00 to 4:00 P.M. daily except Monday, all year.

Den Hirschsprungske Samling (Hirschsprung Collection)

Stockholmsgade 20. Buses 10, 14, 40, and 43. A charming little museum devoted to 19th-century Danish painting, sculpture, and decorative art. Heinrich Hirschsprung, a rich tobacco merchant, donated the works to the Danish state at the turn of the century. Look out for the portraits and pristine landscapes of C.W. Eckersberg (1783–1853), a teacher at Copenhagen's Royal Academy whose meticulous style had a far-reaching influence. The romantic landscapes by Johan Lundbye date from the middle of the 19th century. A generation later, Peter Severin Krøyer worked to popularize social-

realist themes, while a unique Impressionist style was being developed by Laurits Tuxen as a student in Paris. Open Wednesday 11:00 A.M. to 9:00 P.M., Thursday through Monday 11:00 A.M. to 4:00 P.M. Closed Tuesday.

Frihedsmuseet
(Museum of the Danish Resistance)

Churchillparken; buses 1, 6, and 9 from Rådhuspladsen. A graphic record of wartime tragedy and eventual triumph. Every half hour a loudspeaker commentary in Danish and English will guide you round the display. Open May through mid-September Tuesday–Saturday 10:00 A.M. to 4:00 P.M. and Sunday until 5:00 P.M.; mid-September through April Tuesday–Saturday 11:00 A.M. to 3:00 P.M. and Sunday until 4:00 P.M.

Kunstindustrimuseet
(Museum of Decorative Art)

Bredgade 68; buses 1 and 6 from Rådhuspladsen. A large display of European and Oriental handicrafts dating from the Middle Ages to the present housed in 1757 Rococo buildings, a former hospital. There is a splendid garden as well. Open Tuesday–Saturday 10:00 A.M. to 4:00 P.M., Sunday 1:00 to 4:00 P.M.

Københavns Bymuseum
(Copenhagen Museum)

Vesterbrogade 59; buses 6, 16, and 28 from Rådhuspladsen. Founded in 1901, this is a children's favourite, with

Rosenberg Castle's beautiful exterior does not belie the riches to be found within.

its scale model of the city centre (1525–1550). Inside are clothing, signboards, photographs, engravings, and posters from the city's past. Here also lies the **Søren Kierkegaard Samling,** a collection of artefacts connected with the Danish philosopher. Open October through April Tuesday–Sunday 1:00 to 4:00 P.M.; May through September Tuesday–Sunday 10:00 A.M. to 4:00 P.M.

Louis Tussauds Voksmuseum (Wax Museum)

H.C. Andersens Boulevard 22. Wax models of famous Danish and foreign personalities, with light and sound effects. Open 24 April–13 September Monday–Sunday 10:00 A.M. to 11:00 P.M.; rest of the year 10:00 A.M. to 4:00 P.M. daily.

☛ Nationalmuseet (National Museum)

Ny Vestergade 10; buses 1, 2, and 6 from Rådhuspladsen. This is nothing less than a well-organized labyrinth of artefacts ranging from Stone Age Danish rock carvings to Mongolian horseriding equipment and tents. The biggest museum in Scandinavia, it consists of eight separate major collections, varying from prehistoric to modern Danish culture, Egyptian and Classical antiquities, coins and medals, and ethnographical and children's displays. Many have varying hours, so check before you plan your visits.

Visitors will be intrigued to study the prehistoric Denmark that led up to those extraordinary Viking times. Outstanding among Stone Age exhibits here is the Hindsgavle Dagger (1800–1500 B.C.), fashioned out of flint after bronze weapons in use elsewhere. Bronze technology came to Denmark after 1500 B.C., and a wealth of interesting objects from the period are on view. The most striking exhibit is the Sun Chariot of 1200 B.C. The Danes once worshipped the sun, imagining it just as it is here: a disc of gold riding through the sky in a chariot behind a celestial horse.

Through its colonization of Greenland, Danish culture opens doors on to Eskimo culture. The lively exhibition of huskies, igloos, reconstructed Eskimo camps, and medieval clothes preserved in Greenland subsoil (ground floor rooms, Ny Vestergade entrance) is worth a visit. Open year round Tuesday through Sunday 10:00 A.M. to 5:00 P.M. Closed Mondays.

One of three almost life-sized silver lions in the Long Hall at Rosenberg Castle.

Ny Carlsberg Glyptotek

Dantes Plads 7, on H.C. Andersens Boulevard. Buses 1, 2, 5, 8, 10, 14, and 16. A split personality museum with a touch of genius at either end of the psychic range. Basically, the Glyptotek was founded on the Classical collection of Carl Jacobsen, a Danish brewer and art connoisseur (1842–1914), and was then developed by his family. Under its elaborate roof lies one of the world's foremost exhibitions of Egyptian, Greek, Roman, and Etruscan art, with enough statues and artefacts to equip 100 ancient temples. As the museum was specially built around the Classical collection, you'll find unique features like the breathtaking central hall, which appears to be transplanted direct from ancient Rome.

In complete contrast is the other collection: 25 Gauguins, three van Goghs, several Monets, and seven Rodin statues all competing for attention in a compressed, four-room show, with a complete set of Degas bronzes—73 delicate statues which won the painter posthumous acclaim as a sculptor.

Museum open Tuesday–Sunday 10:00 A.M. to 4:00 P.M.; admission free Wednesday and Sunday. Closed Monday.

Rosenborg Slot (Rosenborg Castle)

Øster Vold-gade 4A; buses 14 and 16 from Rådhuspladsen, or S-train to Nørreport. This castle's 10,000 exhibits span Danish royal history over the past 500 years, though outside the dazzling cellar display of crown jewels the focus falls mainly on relics from the founder Christian IV himself.

The castle's 24 rooms are arranged chronologically, beginning with his tower room study—still furnished in original style. The **Long Hall,** with its Swedish Wars tapestries, ornate ceiling, and three almost life-size silver lions, is not to be hurried. In the hall is one of the world's largest collections of silver furniture, most of it from the 18th century.

The treasury, which is in the cellar, is home to the crown jewels. Besides the oldest existing specimen of the Order of the Elephant (see page 49), there are 18 cases full of crowns, gilded swords, precious stones, and coronation cups—even royal inkwells and tea-sets in pure gold. The centrepiece of this regal room is the 17th-century crown of the absolute monarchy—made out of gold, with diamonds, two sapphires, and ruby spinels.

Open March through May and September through the last week in October daily 11:00 A.M. to 3:00 P.M.; and June through August every day 10:00 A.M. to 4:00 P.M.

Statens Museum for Kunst (The National Gallery)

Sølvgade 48-50; bus 10 from Kongens Nytorv and 75E (during rush hours) from Rådhuspladsen. This museum reopened in 1998 after renovations. Fine paintings from early Dutch to modern Danish are housed in one light, airy building. The museum is particularly strong on 19th-century Danish landscapes, Matisse, representative Dutch and Flemish works of art from Rembrandt to Paulus Potter, an Italian collection including Titian and Tintoretto, and perhaps the world's finest collection of Dürer prints. The bold colours employed by the Danish painter Niels Larsen Stevns (1864–1941), one of the great painters of his day, catch the eye. Open all year Tuesday–Sunday 10:00 A.M. to 5:00 P.M., until 9:00 P.M. Wednesday; closed Monday.

Thorvaldsens Museum

Porthusgade 2; buses 1, 2, 6, 8, and 10 from Rådhuspladsen. This is another museum of Classical intent. Roman and Greek gods and goddesses gazing down at you, however, are all 19th-century revivals of antiquity: the work of Bertel Thorvaldsen (1770–1844), the greatest of Danish sculptors and Copenhagen's only honorary citizen.

Returning after 40 years in Rome—the Danish government fetched him back in triumph—he devoted his library, collection, and fortune to the creation of a museum of his own works, choosing a young architect, Gottlieb Bindesbøll, to design it. The result was one of Copenhagen's most distinctive, untypical buildings, with a decorated ochre façade, and interior walls and ceilings in black, reds, blues, and oranges that throw into high contrast the pure white plaster and marble of Thorvaldsen's sculpture.

The ground-floor display in 21 interlinked sections shows why he has been called one of the greatest sculptors since the days of the Caesars—a noble array of chaste Classical gods, popes, and aristocracy, an idealized vision of mankind with never a wart in sight. Open all year round Tuesday–Sunday 10:00 A.M. to 5:00 P.M.; tours 3:00 P.M. on Sunday.

EXCURSIONS

In a country of 44,030 square km (17,000 square miles), nature has ingeniously divided Denmark into more than 450 islands so that you are never more than 50 km (30 miles) from the sea. Copenhageners have their own beach, woodlands, and a wide lake area, and within the city boundary you can easily organize an excursion including a boat trip, windmills and water-mills, a royal country castle, and genuine village settings.

Open-Air Folk Museum and Lyngby Lake

Initially we're aiming for **Frilandsmuseet** (Open-Air Folk Museum) at Sorgenfri, 16 km (10 miles) north of the city, accessible by car along the A3 and A5 main roads, by direct bus 184 from Nørreport terminus in town, or by S-train, line Cc to Sorgenfri station. Another more interesting and adventurous route is to take the same train and change at Jægersborg station to the little red one-coach train known as *Grisen* ("The Pig"), which will drop you at Fuglevad Station near the museum's back entrance.

Forty farmhouses, cottages, workshops, and a Dutch-type windmill are sprinkled about the 36-hectare (90-acre) site of Frilandsmuseet—all furnished in authentic style with everything down to combs and portraits.

Broadly, the buildings are split into geographical groups laid out along country lanes, together with bridges and village pumps, and all authentically landscaped. Each of these has been transplanted, tile by tile, timber by timber, from its original location. You'll find a Zealand group, a Jutland, and a Faroes group, etc. Homes of all classes are represented—from peasant to landowner, as well as artisan and farmer.

The smell of old timber and tar pervades the rooms. Geese and sheep are driven along the lanes. Displays of folk dancing, sheep shearing, threshing, and weaving are given during the summer. There are horse-and-carriage rides, and picnic spots in tree-lined meadows.

Both the opening hours and times of guided tours (in English) tend to change from one year to the next, so before you set out for Frilandsmuseet be sure to refer to the daily press or the Copenhagen tourist information office (see page 125).

Allow yourself time when the weather is fine to stroll half a mile down the main road towards Lyngby and a rural boat ride scarcely equalled in any capital city. On your left is the white-walled Baroque castle, **Sorgenfri Slot** (closed to the public), built in the 18th century by the man who also designed the spire of Vor Frelsers Kirke (see page 48). Proceed over Mølleåaen (the Mill Stream).

Follow signs to the right for *Lyngby Sø—Bådfarten* ("Lyngby Lake—Boat Trip") to find at the quayside two venerable canopied boats that have plied the four lakes since the 1890s.

A 45-minute **cruise,** either Lyngby–Frederiksdal or Lyngby–Sophienholm, gives you a flavour of these delightful tree-covered backwaters and broad, reedy lakes. The boats operate from May to September or October, depending on the weather.

As you float by, you'll pass the 1803 mansion of Marienborg amidst the trees, the official summer residence of Danish prime ministers; farther on is Frederiksdal with its **castle** on a hill above. This former royal house has been lived in by the same family since 1740.

An alternative trip will take you to **Sophienholm Mansion** (1805), now a community cultural arts centre. Outdoor café tables give an idyllic view over the waters of Bagsværd Sø.

Back on Lyngby quay: the 184 bus can take you direct to town again, or it's a short walk to Lyngby S-train station to rejoin the A- or Cc-line service.

A day in the lush Copenhagen countryside is a lovely alternative to consider during your visit.

North Zealand and Its Castles

Some 130 km (around 80 miles) of sea views and castle turrets, beaches, and rolling farmland is what you can expect if you set about touring northern Zealand.

In fine weather you might prefer the drive through the beach suburbs to the north of Copenhagen and along the "Danish Riviera," with its small fishing villages and bays. If you are more pressed for time, head straight up the A3 motorway (or expressway) out of Copenhagen in the direction of Helsingør.

One major attraction just to the south of Humlebæk, accessible from either the A3 or the coast road, is the **Louisiana Modern Art Museum,** housed in the mid-19th-

century mansion of a thrice-married cheese merchant whose wives were all called Louise. The superb gardens are dotted with sculptures, ranging from colossal Henry Moore works to metal mobiles by Alexander Calder. The airy, white interior houses everything from mural-sized Chagalls to special pop-art shows. Open all year round Monday–Friday 10:00 A.M. to 5:00 P.M., till 10:00 P.M. on Wednesday; 10:00 A.M. to 6:00 P.M. weekends.

The **castle** at **Helsingør** (to many of us better known as Elsinore) soon appears within view, jutting out in the direction of Sweden, a striking square of green roofs against the blue Sound.

"Hamlet's castle" is a misnomer, of course. Though Laurence Olivier and Vivien Leigh certainly trod its ancient corridors when making the film of *Hamlet*, the tragic prince himself never slept here and it is probable that Shakespeare derived the name from Amleth (or Amled), a Jutland prince of pre-Viking times.

The real name of the castle is Kronborg. It was built between 1574 and 1585 at the command of King Frederik II for the purpose of extracting tolls from ships that were entering the narrow Sound (and thus the Baltic) at this point.

Frederik had more than just a stronghold in mind. He built a castle that could be lived in, fortified with ramparts and bastions so a number of large windows and decorated towers could be added with impunity. He sent for Flemish architect Antonius van Opbergen to design the four-wing structure, then engaged various Danish and Dutch artists to paint, weave, and indulge in decorative sculpture on a scale never before seen in Scandinavia.

Kronborg Castle may be better known to some as Elsinore, though Hamlet himself never slept here.

Fredensborg Castle: where King Frederik V played and the royal family still stays.

Restored this century, the moated brick castle today stands as Frederik's proudest memorial, now sparsely furnished but immensely impressive. It has a feel of solid strength and royal presence throughout, permeating the elaborate little **chapel,** the long galleries and the stone stairways, and most of all the huge oak-beamed **Banqueting Hall.** At 64 by 11 metres (210 by 36 feet), it is the largest hall of its kind in northern Europe and one of the noblest rooms of the Danish Renaissance. Decked out now with twelve paintings of the Sound by Isaac Isaacsz, its white walls were once hung with 42 famous tapestries by the Dutchman Hans Knieper, depicting the 111 Danish kings said to have reigned before Frederik II. Fourteen of the tapestries still survive, of which seven are to be seen in a small room beneath the hall, and the remainder in the National Museum (see page 60). Underneath the castle are extensive casements and dungeons. The most famous exhibit at Kronborg, however, is the statue of Holger the Dane (see page 10).

In the castle's northern wing you'll discover the interesting **Handels-og Søfartsmuseet** (Trade and Maritime Museum) with its display of navigation instruments, as well as relics from early Danish settlements in Greenland and elsewhere.

The castle and museum are open daily except Mondays, May through September 10:00 A.M. to 5:00 P.M., November through March 11:00 A.M. to 3:00 P.M., April and October 11:00 A.M. to 4:00 P.M.; guided tours every half hour.

After perhaps stopping for a coffee at one of the numerous cafés on Helsingør's 18th-century marketplace, keep going along the northern coast road to Dronningmølle, which has one of the best beaches on the Kattegat, before turning south in the direction of Esrum for a cross-sectional view of rural Zealand: winding lanes, beech forests, farmland cultivated to the road edge, and traditional farmsteads built with four wings surrounding a cobbled courtyard. At Esrum, follow the signs via Jonstrup and drive along the Esrum Sø to the castle lying on the water's edge, **Fredensborg Slot.**

Erected between 1719 and 1722, Fredensborg is an excellent example of Italian/Dutch Baroque, set on a small

Frederiksborg Castle, surrounded by water, stretches dramatically across three islands.

You can visit the cathedral at Roskilde (Domkirken) free if you buy a special Roskilde train ticket—it's worth the trip.

hill, surrounded by grounds that were the delight of King Frederik V, who turned this hunting seat into a royal summer residence. He held great parties here, and had statues installed in the lakeside grounds—not of his peers but of ordinary people, with exact renderings of the folk costumes. You can stroll the grounds any time, but the royal apartments and the private garden are open only in the royal family's absence.

Continue for a further 9 km (5½ miles) as far as Hillerød and the site of Denmark's architectural showpiece, Christian IV's grandest achievement, and one of the greatest Renaissance castles in northern Europe: **Frederiksborg Slot,** a brick-and-sandstone castle dramatically sited across three islands. During the years of the absolutist kings, every single Danish monarch was anointed and crowned here.

In 1859 much of the interior was destroyed by fire. Twenty years later a plan put forward by the brewer J.C. Jacobsen to restore the castle into a Danish Versailles—a museum of national history—was approved by royal ordinance. Spanning more than 60 rooms of the castle, there is today a complete record of the Danish monarchy, beginning with Christian I, who established the Oldenburg line (1448–1863), through all the monarchs of the following Glücksburg line, right down to the present queen.

Riddersalen (the Knights' Hall) and the chapel are Frederiksborg's ultimate triumph. The 56-metre (185-foot) Knights' Hall is awesome in its dimensions, with tapestried walls, marble floor, and carved wooden ceiling, all reconstructed from old drawings after the 1859 fire.

Below the Knights' Hall, **Slotskirken** (the chapel) escaped the fire, with its stunning gilt pillars and high vaulted nave virtually untouched. Almost every inch here is richly carved and ornamented. The chapel has inset black-marble panels with scriptural quotes, marquetry panels in ebony and rare woods, and both its altar and pulpit in ebony with biblical scenes in silver relief. The **organ** is one of Europe's most notable, an almost unchanged original from 1610 by Flemish master Esaias Compenius.

Around the gallery of this chapel the window piers and recesses are hung with coats-of-arms belonging to knights of both the orders of the Elephant and the Grand Cross of Danneborg. Some modern recipients are also represented, such as Sir Winston Churchill and General Eisenhower.

After a short stroll around the cobbled courtyards, perhaps pausing for a rest beside the 1620 **Neptune Fountain,** return to Copenhagen, 32 km (20 miles) back along the A5.

Frederiksborg Castle is only open in July, daily 1:00 to 5:00 P.M. The Baroque gardens are open at 10:00 A.M. year-round, closing at different hours according to the season. Without a car, it can be reached by regular S-train service to Hillerød;

then from the centre of Hillerød the Frederiksborg Ferry plies across the lake towards the castle. Sightseeing tours starting from Copenhagen are also available during most of the year.

☞ Roskilde

With an 800-year-old cathedral housing the splendid tombs of 37 monarchs, with Viking ships salvaged from the fjord and now presented in a unique maritime museum, with young scientists welcoming visitors to their nearby prehistoric village. Having just celebrated its 1,000-year anniversary in 1998, Roskilde has plenty to offer those who undertake the brief (30-minute) journey from Copenhagen centre.

Whether you go by car, bus, or train, make straight for the centre of this small, neat town and for the three green spires which dominate the flat landscape for miles about. This is **Domkirken** (the Cathedral), begun as a wooden church by King Harald Bluetooth around 1000 when he was converted to Christianity. In the 1170s, Bishop Absalon, founder of Copenhagen (see page 12), built a brick-and-stone cathedral here for his new bishopric, and during the course of the next 300 years this grew into the Romanesque-Gothic amalgam of today. Christian IV added the distinctive spires in 1635. He also erected his own burial chapel and a gilded royal pew in the north wall of the church, heavily latticed and shielded from public view so that (it is said) he could smoke his pipe in peace during Sunday services. Nearly all the Danish kings and queens since Margrete (d. 1412) are buried here.

The sarcophagi and chapels are all different from one another, a jumbled symphony of style. On the south side, the chapel of King Frederik V is simple in white paint and Norwegian marble, with 12 tombs grouped around it. In contrast, the Christian IV chapel on the north side is marked by elaborately wrought ironwork from 1618 and interior decoration mainly from the 19th century.

A light note is introduced by the clock high on the southwest wall of the nave. As each hour arrives, St. George and his horse rear up, beneath them a dragon utters a shrill cry, and a woman figure strikes her little bell four times with a hammer, a man his big bell once.

The chapel on the outside of the cathedral beside the northwestern tower was inaugurated in 1985 and dedicated to the memory of Frederik IX, King of Denmark from 1947 to 1972, who is buried here.

To the front of the church is Stændertorvet, the traditional square of this old market town, lined with outdoor café tables in good weather, and fruit and vegetable stalls every Wednesday and Saturday morning. On Saturday there is also a popular flea market. To the rear is some public parkland, where you can walk down to the fjord and **Vikingeskibshallen** (the Viking Ship Museum).

Vikingeskibshallen houses five 11th-century Viking ships, plus other exhibits illuminating this amazing find.

When 11th-century Danes wanted to block off the sea-route to Roskilde from the ravaging Norwegians, they sank five Viking ships across a narrow neck of the shallow fjord here. These ships, salvaged in 1962, now form the basis of the Viking Ship Museum. The museum building stands on the edge of the water with one side completely glass, bringing the fjord almost into its main room. The outline of each ship was first reconstructed in metal strips, then the thousands of pieces of wood were placed in position after treatment.

The museum is lavishly illustrated with photographs and charts, and free film shows are put on for the public in the cinema-cellar, recounting in English the full story of the salvage.

Roskilde is a go-ahead town offering lively entertainment, with open-air theatre and fjord boat trips in summer, concerts and cattle shows, bonfires and fireworks. If you are going by train, ask at Copenhagen Station for the special Roskilde ticket (*Roskilde særtilbud*), a package including entrance to the cathedral and ship museum as well as your return rail fare.

Continue 10 km (6 miles) southwest, by Lejre, to reach the Historical-Archaeological Research Centre **Oldtidsbyen** (Ancient Town). Here a group of enthusiasts are not only living in Iron-Age style, in clay and reed houses that look like a cluster of shaggy dogs, but are actually in the throes of a major long-term scientific experiment in which they are attempting to trace the effect on the environment of primitive man's use of tools, examining how his needs and life-style destroyed or added to the natural amenities, and how forest and wildlife disappeared.

Every year 80,000 visitors flock to Lejre to see the farm, the workshops, the explanatory films in Danish and English, and for the curiously reincarnated prehistoric houses with their smoky interiors and primitive living conditions.

The village is open May through September daily 10:00 A.M. to 5:00 P.M., but is closed in winter.

WHAT TO DO

SHOPPING

Shopping in Copenhagen is a quality experience, and the city's pedestrianized precincts and attractive squares add to the pleasure of seeking out that special purchase. A host of interesting shops in the pleasant side streets and shopping arcades around the Strøget area specialize in everything from antiques to avant-garde furniture, while established department stores such as Illum and Magasin du Nord offer the very best in Danish design.

Shopping Hours

Shops are generally open from 10:00 A.M. until 5:30 P.M. Monday through Friday; Danish shopping hours have recently been legally extended in morning and evening on the weekdays. A small number of shops (often food shops) are closed on Mon-

Copenhagen's pedestrian- and bicycle-friendly streets make shopping a very pleasant experience.

The Copenhagen Jazz Festival takes to the water.

day or Tuesday. Saturday hours are 9:00 A.M. to 1:00 or 2:00 P.M.

Certain shops stay open longer. These include bakeries, florists, *smørrebrød* shops, and kiosks. In addition, late-night (until 10:00 P.M. or midnight) and Sunday shopping is possible at the Central Station, which is like a cheery village with a supermarket, banks open for foreign exchange, a post office, room-booking service, and snack bars. There are also several central 24-hour shops (look for the sign *dag og nat shop*) selling fresh bread from 3:00 A.M. onwards plus other food, beer, and spirits.

Where to Shop

The linked, completely pedestrianized streets of Strøget/Fiolstræde/Købmagergade have it all: the finest ceramics and silver shops, perhaps the best art-household stores in the world, the city's leading furriers, antiques shops by the score (also found in some smaller streets branching off), workshops belonging to young potters and silversmiths, shops for clothes and knitwear, toys, and pipes, and dozens of souvenir shops and kiosks.

Slightly more off the beaten track—unless you're visiting Amalienborg and the Marble Church—is Bredgade/Store Kongensgade, with its extensive range of boutiques.

Sales tax, or VAT (in Danish *MOMS*), is 25 percent on all products and services. This tax will be refunded to foreign visitors who make large purchases (above 600kr) in outlets that display "Tax-Free Shopping" stickers. Ask for details in the shop. (See page 121.)

Good Buys

Amber jewellery is on offer everywhere, particularly in the shops along Strøget. The local "gem" (actually fossil resin), from the southern Baltic, may be cheaper here than at home.

Antiques are in plentiful supply, especially the home-spun rather than the fine-art variety. The most likely shops to try are in the Old Town area.

Aquavit (*akvavit*), the local spirit, usually flavoured with caraway seed, is cheaper than imported spirits. The best prices are at airport duty-free.

Danish porcelain. The secret of its poetic effect is an underglaze technique shared only by Royal Copenhagen Porcelain (founded in 1775) and Bing & Grøndahl (1853) which allows landscape pastels, and even accurate skin colours, to be reproduced. Blue motifs come out particularly well. All the pieces from these companies are hand-painted after a quick first firing, then fired again for glazing at 1,400°C (2,600°F). No two pieces are alike. They range from ashtrays to dinner services, with prices to match.

The stylized and highly decorative ceramics of the contemporary Danish artist Bjørn Wiinblad are highly popular, while avant-garde and classic European designs are available from Rosenthal Studio-Haus at Frederiksberggade 21 near Rådhuspladsen.

Glassware and stainless steel household products are especially good buys to take home if you want top quality design matched with excellent craftsmanship. There is still a

thriving tradition of blown glass, and at Hinz/Kjær Glasdesign in Pistolstræde you can watch skilled craftsmen at work on their exquisite and colourful creations.

Stereo equipment. The very latest in stereo systems, CD players, radios, and TV sets can be found at the Bang & Olufsen Center, Østergade 3-5, near to Kongens Nytorv.

Household furnishings. Danish furniture ranks among the world's best. Here you'll see items credited to the designer rather than to the factory. Furniture is a national pride and most good pieces will have a black circular "Danish Furniture-Makers' Control" sticker attached. Lamps are also a lovingly designed product, as are household textiles and hand-woven rugs. The best shops for interior furnishings are Illums Bolighus on Strøget and Tre Falke Møbler in the

Entertainment in the city of Copenhagen ranges from the sublime beauty of the Royal Danish Ballet (left) to the hard-hitting exuberance of the Jazz Festival (above).

Falkoner Centre on Falkoner Allé. Look out, too, for tradition-al Danish eiderdowns and duvets; Ofelia in Strøget Arcade off Vimmelskaftet offers an excellent and varied selection.

Knitwear comes Nordic-style, often highly patterned, warm, and in some cases expensive. There are knitwear shops all over the city; some sell wool and patterns for those who are tempted to set about knitting their own garments.

Silver is another Danish speciality, dominated by the name Georg Jensen. Silver in Denmark is quality-controlled and should always be hallmarked. The Jensen showrooms at Amagertorv 4 offer creations that range from key rings to highly precious jewellery.

Souvenirs are myriad. Little mermaid figures, Copen-hagen dolls in frilly skirts and black lace caps, blue ceramic figurines and animals, and countless trolls and Vikings abound, as well as hand-painted spoons, racks, and pepper-mills. A particularly attractive Danish keepsake is an Am-ager shelf—a group of three or four small hand-painted shelves in a triangular frame that hangs on the wall. Beware, however, of cheap versions.

Toys are simple and attractive, especially those in solid wood. You'll also see hundreds of the Danish wooden sol-diers in all sizes. Many new shops such as Krea have opened up which specialize in educational toys for chil-dren of all ages.

Festivals

Denmark has no great religious festivals or processions, and few spectacular state ceremonies. Yet festivities of some kind are in the air all the time, and a glance at *Copenhagen This Week* (see page 119) will give you an idea of just how many. The following summary gives a flavour of what to expect during the year:

St. John's Eve: *Sankt Hansaften* (June 23). Bonfires are lit all along the "Riviera" coastline north of Copenhagen to drive the witches away on their broomsticks to Blocksberg in Germany.

Viking Festival: *Vikingespil* (mid-June to early July). Plays, mead, and barbecues at Frederikssund (bus tours available).

Copenhagen Summer Festival: Pop concerts and chamber music in different parts of the city; admission is free.

Roskilde Festival (late June to early July): Greatest pop fes-tival in northern Europe—jazz and rock in a delightful setting.

Copenhagen Jazz Festival (mid July): International jazz.

Copenhagen Choir Festival (late October): Choral events.

ENTERTAINMENT

When in Copenhagen, relax as the Danes do. Hire a bike for a different view of life, stroll the beech woods and parks, have a night on the town at a concert or jazz club—or simply pause for a snack on one of the many public benches.

Beaches. Bellevue Beach is a mere 20 minutes' journey away by S-train (line C) to Klampenborg—so easy, you'll join in a city exodus on sunny days.

Botanical gardens. Keen gardeners could happily pass two or three days examining the 70 laid-out areas, the palm house and various other greenhouses on the 10-hectare (25-acre) Botanisk Have site opposite Rosenborg Castle. It remains open year-round till sunset. Get there by bus 14 from Rådhuspladsen, or alternatively buses 7 and 17 from Kongens Nytorv.

Café society. Another way of life altogether—relaxed, welcoming. Sit as long as you like over a beer or coffee, let yourself gaze at the eccentric décor, and take time out to meet the Danes. There are several especially friendly bars in the area around the university.

Cycling. Some hotels lend bicycles free to their guests. Otherwise they're easy to hire (see page 104). Once you're perched on a saddle, the world is your oyster. Ride the extensive network of cycle paths *(cykelsti)* without any worry about cars, or indeed the weather—if it decides to rain, country buses will pack your bike on the top. Taxis also have bicycle racks.

Nightlife

Music, opera, ballet: Scores of concerts are held all year at the Royal Theatre, Tivoli, the Royal Conservatory of Music, Radio House, in churches, and in museums. The Royal Dan-

Up, up, and away: there are myriad ways to amuse yourself at Tivoli.

ish Ballet is a world-renowned organization, and rightly so; it is one of Europe's oldest, their repertory having a 200-year history. Nowadays, the company experiments in modern dance as well, but its great tradition lies in Bournonville classics, which are worth trying to go to see. The Ballet performs from September through June only.

Jazz, folk, rock: Copenhagen has been called Europe's leading jazz centre. Various main clubs offer jazz for all persuasions every night until 2:00 A.M. or later. Many foreign stars now live in Denmark and appear at leading clubs, such as Club Montmartre in Nørregade. At smaller bars the jazz is free. There are four venues for folk music in the downtown area, near the university. Rock music events frequently appear in the regular Copenhagen listings. On summer Sundays there are free rock concerts held in Fælled Park.

Nightclubs: There is a plethora of late-opening bars that serve as nightclubs, with the emphasis firmly on entertainment.

Discos: The usual routine for entrance into a Copenhagen disco is to enroll as a member at the door. Almost every variety of dance hall, from downbeat discotheques to sophisticated hotel nightclubs, are readily available, easy to find, and welcoming to visitors.

Cinemas: Films are shown in their original language with Danish subtitles.

At home: If you are fortunate enough to be invited to a Danish home, make sure you grab the chance. The Danes love to entertain and set great store by creating a cosy yet chic atmosphere for their guests.

Copenhagen by night: Copenhagen is, of course, well known for its more risqué entertainment and red-light district. This is now located in the rather unobtrusive Istedgade/ Halmtorvet area to the west of the Central Station.

SPORTS

There's plenty of sporting activities for every type within easy reach of the city. The top spectator sport is football (soccer), while popular participation sports are sailing and fishing. Ask the nearest Danish tourist office (see page 125) for an up-to-date list of all facilities, or contact the Copenhagen Sports Centre (Idrættens Hus), tel. 43 26 26 26.

Bungee jumping. This daring activity has recently taken off internationally, and in Copenhagen you can practise it in the safety of the harbour.

Fishing. Jutland is the Danish mecca for sea fishing, but you can still go for Øresund cod, mackerel, gar-pike, or flatfish from Amager and the coast to the north of the city. No special permit is required for fishing in Denmark, either in its lakes or rivers—a real boost to anglers. You can hire licensed boats on Lyngby, Furesø, and Bagsværd lakes on the northwest edge of Copenhagen.

Football (soccer). The Danish football team competes at the highest level, and the sport has an enthusiastic following. Amateur games are played every weekend from April to

Wind-surfing and other watersports are popular pastimes on the summer seas of Copenhagen.

June and August to November, and certain weekday afternoons in May, June, and September. The main Copenhagen stadium is at Idrætsparken.

Golf. Always an option, with at least 129 clubs in Denmark, and 8 within 40 km (25 miles) of Copenhagen, the nearest being in Klampenborg suburb at Dyrehaven 2, tel. 39 63 04 83. Green fees are moderate throughout Denmark, and foreigners are welcomed.

Horse-racing. Also at Klampenborg, the racing track *(galopbane)* opens mainly Saturdays from mid-April to mid-December. Take the S-train to Klampenborg, then take bus 160.

Horseback riding. Good riding, especially in the Deer Park. There are several stables and schools in the area; for details look in the *Fagbog* (a telephone directory to trade and professions) under *Rideundervisning*.

Rowing. A major sporting activity, with an Olympic course and many clubs—details available from the Danish Rowing Association *(Dansk Forening for Rosport)*, Vester Voldgade 91, 1552 Copenhagen V.

Sailing. Join the Sound and inland lake throngs. Yachts and cruisers are available for hire. Evidence of navigational proficiency is required for sailing on the Øresund, where a close watch must be kept out for the constant ferry traffic. Book in advance with help from your local Danish tourist office.

Skating. Numerous stretches of water within the city boundaries freeze up in winter. There are also indoor rinks *(skøjtehal)* at Copenhagen Forum and other suburban locations. All open October through April.

Swimming. There is good sea bathing along the whole of the Zealand coast north and south of the city, but the sea is rarely warm. Nude bathing is mainly at Tisvildeleje, away from the north coast. There are about a dozen indoor swimming baths in Copenhagen, some of these with sauna/massage and gym facilities, and several outdoor pools which open from mid-May until the end of August.

Tennis. For a small fee, you can obtain guest membership of local clubs. Foreign players are welcome, though advance booking is necessary. Contact the tourist office for addresses.

Watersports. Water-skiing is popular on the Furesø, and it is possible to windsurf in Vedbæk harbour; contact Vedbæk Surfer Club, tel. 215 66 01 18, or try consulting the tourist office for details.

CHILDREN'S COPENHAGEN

Amusement parks. Tivoli, of course, should certainly appeal to the whole family. Another really fun place for children is **Bakken,** 10 km (6 miles) north of Copenhagen on the edge of the Deer Park (Dyrehaven; see below). It's older than Tivoli and slightly less sophisticated, with a big dipper and beer hall, circus revue and hall of distorting mirrors, a bingo and pantomime, a children's play park (look for *børnelegeplads*), funfairs, dodgems, and a wide choice of eating establishments. While you are here take the opportunity to try the *æbleskiver som vor mor bager dem*, "apple slices like mother makes" (deep-fried in batter). Open during the summer; entrance is free.

Circus. Lying almost opposite Tivoli, down Axeltorv. Established in 1887 and voted the best circus in continental Europe for four years in a row. It holds shows every night, from May to October.

Dyrehaven. To one side of the rail station for Bellevue Beach you'll find the entrance to the Royal Deer Park, now open to all and stretching for miles. Go along by horse and carriage to watch the deer feeding. Make sure, however, to check carefully on the prices.

Museums and attractions. A likely hit with the children is Legoland, featuring exhibits such as a working boat and a scaled-down Statue of Liberty made entirely out of Legos. Other favourite children's attractions include: Ripley's Believe it or Not! museum at Rådhuspladsen 57, a motley collection of "bizarre but true" exhibits; the Tycho Brahe Planetarium, Gammel Kongevej 10, with its space theatre and star shop; the Ecksperimentarium science centre, Tuborg Havnevej 7, Hellerup, where the kids are positively encouraged to tinker around with exhibits; and the Aquarium, Charlottenlund, a home to more than 3,000 varieties of aquatic life, including bloodthirsty piranhas.

Tours. Almost anything to do with water appeals to youngsters, and organized canal trips are a must. Also worth considering are the boat cruises that depart from Roskilde harbour. Among farther-flung options are a coach tour to Legoland in Jutland, and a train journey to Fantasy World in South Zealand, with the chance thrown in to catch a glimpse of Santa Claus. Contact the tourist office for details of these and other tours.

Zoo. Copenhagen's Zoologisk Have, one of the finest in Europe, has been around for over 120 years. It plays host to more than 2,500 animals, and has a splendid children's section, restaurant, and cafeteria. It is open all year from 9:00 A.M. to sunset or to 6:00 P.M. at the latest; Roskildevej 32, only a 10-minute ride from Rådhuspladsen by buses 28 and 39.

Legoland is no less than a fantasy destination for children the world over.

EATING OUT

Food is of a high standard in Denmark, and counts as little short of an obsession. Danes at home will happily spend two hours over their *frokost* (lunch) or up to four if entertaining special guests, whilst a dinner (*middag*) in celebratory mood can last from 6:00 P.M. to infinity.

Restaurants and Bars

There are more than 2,000 assorted restaurants, cafés, bars, and snack bars in Copenhagen. Restaurants often serve a special dish of the day (*dagens ret*) and what is known as the "Dan-menu"—a two-course Danish lunch or dinner for a fixed price—in addition to à la carte items. Keep an eye open for a *daglig kort* ("daily card"), which usually features less expensive dishes than those listed on the more formal menu (*spisekort*). You'll also find little lunch-only, cosy cellar restaurants listed in *Copenhagen This Week* (see page 119). These offer good value with an Old-World charm, and are well frequented by Danes themselves. Out of town, a *kro* (country inn) can provide a charming if occasionally expensive setting for a special meal.

Soak up the beautiful weather at one of Copenhagen's sidewalk cafés.

For a drink in the evening (or in fact practically any time of the day or night—opening hours are particularly liberal), drop into one of the numerous cafés, pubs, or bars that are dotted throughout the city. One traditional Danish drinking establishment is the *værtshus*, which will be tidy or tatty according to its neighbourhood.

Value-added tax and service charge are included in the bill. Danes are not tip-minded, although after a meal you may want to round up your bill.

Breakfast

Breakfast (*morgenmad*) in a Danish hotel is a far cry from the Spartan "Continental breakfast" of a roll and a cup of coffee. Bread rolls, meat, cheese, jam, pastries, and possibly an egg are all accompanied by a glass of milk or fruit juice followed by tea or coffee.

Cold Dishes

Cold food is Denmark's truly outstanding culinary speciality, which you can soon learn to enjoy. *Smørrebrød* are thickly buttered slices of rye or white bread covered with one of a wide array of delicacies: liver pâté (*leverpostej*), beef tartare (*bøf tartar*), veal (*kalvekød*), ham (*skinke*), roast beef (*roast beef*), salmon (*laks*), smoked eel (*røget ål*), shrimp (*rejer*), cod roe (*torskerogn*), herring (*sild*), salad (*salat*), or cheese (*ost*). This main layer is garnished with a variety of accessories that have been carefully chosen to enhance both taste and appearance. Larger restaurants have scores of different *smørrebrød*. The usual procedure is to tick off your orders on the menu itself, specifying which kind of bread you want (*knækbrød*: crispbread; *rugbrød*: rye; *franskbrød*: white; *pumpernikkel*: black). Two or three of these substantial "open sandwiches" will generally satisfy most appetites.

However, just to give you an idea, one Copenhagen restaurant offers 178 varieties of *smørrebrød*.

Don't confuse your *smørrebrød* with the Swedish word *smörgåsbord* which has gained international currency as a description of the pan-Scandinavian cold buffet-style spread, better known in Denmark as the *koldt bord* ("cold table"). Larger restaurants especially will offer a bewildering array of dishes in their *koldt bord*. For a fixed price, you start at one end of the table, helping yourself to herring in various preparations, seafood, mayonnaise salads, and other delicacies, and go on to sample liver pâté, ham, and other cuts of meat. Despite its name, a *koldt bord* always includes a few hot items, such as meat balls, pork sausages, soup, and fried potatoes. Several kinds of bread and salads are also provided.

En platte is a cold dish (a smaller version of *koldt bord*) made up of six to eight specialities, which is often eaten at lunchtime. Danish *akvavit* (see page 97) and beer go especially well with a *koldt bord*.

Fish and Shellfish

Fish (or small canapés) is the traditional first course of a full meal. It is also available individually, of course, and a great variety of fish appear on the Danish menu. Herring is one of the firm favourites, and may be served pickled, marinated, or fried, with a Sherry, vinegar, curry, or fennel dressing. Succulent red Greenland shrimp are also very popular. Lobster is widely on offer—though it is not cheap—as are crab, cod, and halibut.

Plaice features frequently in the local cuisine and may be served boiled or fried with a garnish of shellfish or parsley. You'll see the little Øresund *rødspætte* (red-spot plaice) on every menu. In summer, a speciality is *danske rejer,* small pink shrimp from local waters that are served piled high on white bread.

Eel is a speciality during the winter months, when it is usually fried and served in a white sauce with creamy boiled potatoes and lashings of sliced lemon; or, salted eel may be boiled and served with horseradish.

One great Scandinavian delicacy is *gravad laks,* in which raw salmon is pressed with salt and a small amount of sugar, and then sprinkled generously with chopped dill; a cold sauce of oil, mustard, and sugar is traditionally served alongside as an accompaniment.

The best fish restaurants in Copenhagen are to be found in the Gammel Strand area.

A fine meal and a view of the city from the Radisson SAS Royal Hotel.

Meat and Poultry

Although Danish meat dishes most frequently make use of pork and veal, beef has made a major breakthrough, as Danish farmers now breed more cattle. The kinds of steak that you are most likely to be offered are *fransk bøf,* fillet steak served with herb butter and chips (French fries), and *engelsk bøf,* fillet steak served with fried onions and potatoes. Note that lamb is available only from May to September.

The top restaurants cook in classic French style. In small establishments, however, some typical Danish hot dishes remain; *mørbradbøf* is a delectable legacy of the pork-only days

A visit to an English-style pub will probably cure anyone's homesickness.

—small cuts of what is called tenderloin in English, lean, very tasty, and served as a main course with boiled potatoes, onions, and gravy.

More ordinary fare—but tasty nevertheless—are Danish meatballs (*frikadeller*), a finely minced mixture of pork and veal, often served with potato salad and red cabbage. *Biksemad* is also cheap and tasty: a Danish hash of diced potatoes, meat, and onions with a fried egg on top. *Hakkebøf* is the crumbling Danish hamburger, while *pariserbøf* is a slightly cooked, almost raw, hamburger topped with egg yolk, raw onion, capers, and horseradish. A hearty Danish stew is *Hvids labskovs*, made from chunks of beef boiled with potatoes, peppercorns, and bay leaves.

Chicken is most often served roasted with potatoes fried in butter and a cucumber salad (*agurkesalat*). Turkey is less commonly found on Danish menus, but may be served roasted or boiled as one of a selection of lunchtime dishes. Roast duck comes with apple or prune stuffing and is usually accompanied by caramelized potatoes and a generous array of vegetables.

Salads

The word for salad, *salat*, has two meanings. It can be the familiar side-dish of fresh lettuce, tomato, sliced egg, and plentiful red peppers; or, more often, it's one of several mayonnaise mixtures that are eaten on *smørrebrød* or as an appetizer. *Italiensk salat* consists of diced carrots, asparagus, peas, and macaroni. *Skinkesalat* is basically chopped ham, while *sildesalat* comprises marinated or pickled herring, beetroot, apple, and pickles. These are only the most common of numerous sandwich salads generally available.

Cheese and Fruit

Danish Blue (*Danablu*), a rich, sharp-flavoured cheese, has always had a strong international following. *Mycella* is fairly similar in taste, but is milder. *Fynbo* and *Samsø*, both relatively mild and firm cheeses, possess a sweetish, almost nutty flavour.

Fruit will always come after the cheese platter if you're eating out. Although the greater part of the country's fruit is imported, Denmark can boast a wide range of berries.

Desserts

It will have been obvious from the very start that Denmark is not a good place for dieting. And by the time you get your Danish desserts your best intentions will have been quite

---

Skål! ...and tak!

Learn to say *skål* (the vowel is between "loll" and "hall") with your beer or *akvavit*. It's more than just Danish for "cheers"—it's a ritual if you are invited to a Danish home. Your host usually has privilege of first toast, and will raise a glass, point it towards everyone in turn, looking directly at them—and say *skål*. After all have taken a sip or a swallow, the host will look at each again in turn before putting down the glass.

After the meal itself, the appropriate—and essential—thing to say is *tak for mad* (which is pronounced "tak for maad"), meaning, very simply, "thanks for the meal."

---

definitely routed. Your dessert will almost certainly be laced with cream (*fløde*) or whipped cream (*flødeskum*).

Favourite desserts include: *æblekage* (stewed apples with vanilla, served with alternating layers of biscuit crumbs and topped with whipped cream); also, *bondepige med slør* (a mixture of rye-bread crumbs, apple sauce, sugar, and the ubiquitous whipped cream).

Snacks

For a snack with a difference, try the deep-fried Camembert cheese served with toast and strawberry jam (*ristet franskbrø med friturestegt camembert og jordbærsyltetøj*).

The university area is good for cheap goulashes, hashes, chicken, and *håndmadder* (usually three slender *smørrebrød* with different toppings). Hot-dog stands (*pølsevogn*) may be found everywhere, serving red Danish sausages (*pølse*) with mustards and relishes.

Oddly enough, Danish pastry is known here as Viennese pastry (*wienerbrød*). This distinctive light and flaky delight

---

Beer: Bottles and Cans

Beer, *øl* (draught beer is called *fadøl*), is rather expensive in Denmark, but it is much cheaper when purchased from a retail outlet. Supermarkets and other stores are open until 5:30pm on weekdays and 2pm on Saturday, although some smaller shops do stay open until 8 or 9pm during the week. Technically, it is illegal to sell beer outside these hours and on Sunday and public holidays, though some of the smaller shops turn a blind eye to the law. Don't expect to see cans; for environmental reasons, these are not used in Denmark. Remember there is a deposit for each bottle, which may be refunded by any store.

can be found in any *konditori,* and makes a delectable snack in the middle of the morning or afternoon.

Drinks

Golden Danish **lager** comes in several types: *lys pilsner* (light lager) which has only 2 percent alcohol; the more normal green-bottle *pilsner*; and finally the stouts and special beers (like *elefantøl*) at 6 to 7 percent or more. *Pilsner* is available everywhere almost 24 hours a day. In cafés it costs three or four times the shop price. The rarer draught beer (*fadøl*) is less fizzy and slightly cheaper.

Akvavit is fiery Danish schnaps made from potatoes, often with a caraway taste. The colour varies according to the herbs and spices that have been used for flavouring. It is taken at mealtimes during the opening fish course or with the cheese, and will sometimes be washed down with a beer chaser. If you order *akvavit* with your meal, the bottle may occasionally be put on the table for you to help yourself. Don't be deluded into thinking you'll only be charged for a single measure—back in the bar they'll know exactly how much has gone.

There is also an increasingly popular **non-alcoholic beer,** recently introduced, looking and tasting like pilsner and costing the same.

All **wines** are imported, and while there is a wide selection of French, German, and Italian varieties, they are always rather expensive in restaurants. Even cheap house-wine (*husets vin*) may be three times the supermarket price. After your dinner, try Danish cherry liqueur, *Cherry Heering*.

Coffee (*kaffe*) can be found everywhere, rich, strong, and served with cream. The price may seem high, but the waiter will usually come round offering refills. On a chilly day you might like to try *varm kakao med flødeskum*—a hot cocoa with whipped cream.

To Help You Order ...

Could we have a table?		**Må vi få et bord?**	
Do you have a set menu?		**Har De en dagens ret?**	
I'd like a/an/some ...		**Jeg vil gerne have ...**	
beer	**en øl**	napkin	**en serviet**
bread	**brød**	pepper	**peber**
coffee	**kaffe**	potatoes	**kartofler**
dessert	**en dessert**	salad	**en salat**
fish	**fisk**	salt	**salt**
glass	**et glas**	soup	**suppe**
ice-cream	**is**	sugar	**sukker**
meat	**kød**	tea	**te**
menu	**et spisekort**	vegetables	**grønsager**
milk	**mælk**	(iced) water	**(is) vand**
mustard	**sennep**	wine	**vin**

...and Read the Menu

agurkesalat	cucumber salad	**kål**	cabbage
blomkål	cauliflower	**lagkage**	layer cake
citron	lemon	**lever**	liver
flæskesteg	roast pork and crackling	**løg**	onion
		medisterpølse	pork sausage
grøn peber	green pepper	**nyrer**	kidney
grønne bønner	French beans	**oksekød**	beef
gulerødder	carrots	**pommes frites**	French fries
hamburgerryg	loin of pork	**porrer**	leeks
hindbær	raspberries	**rødkål**	red cabbage
jordbær	strawberries	**svinekød**	pork
kartoffelmos	mashed potatoes	**søtunge**	sole
kirsebær	cherries	**æble**	apple
kotelet	chop	**æg**	egg
kylling	chicken	**æggekage**	omelette

INDEX

HANDY TRAVEL TIPS

An A–Z Summary of Practical Information

A

ACCOMMODATION *(hotel; indlogering)*
(See also CAMPING, YOUTH HOSTELS, and the list of
RECOMMENDED HOTELS starting on page 131)

Danish tourist offices will provide you with extensive lists of hotels and pensions. There is no star system of rating, but the lists
give an indication of various facilities (with bath, restaurant,
number of beds, etc.). Combine this information with the prices
listed, and you get a fair indication of quality. Ask your tourist
office, too, for details of special low rates in off-season. They
can be down by as much as 50%. Rates on page 106 are aver-
ages for double rooms in high season. Service charges and taxes
are included. Single rooms are generally about 30–40% cheaper.

If you arrive in Copenhagen without a room, try the room-
booking service at the tourist information centre, Bernstorffsgade 1, tel. 33 11 13 25, fax 33 93 49 69; expect to pay a small
fee. The tourist bureau, located directly across from the Central
railway Station, is open 9am to 9pm.

"Mission Hotels" *(missionshotel)* are reasonably priced and
popular with Danish family visitors. They are classified as tem-
perance hotels, but will sell wine and beer to guests. There are
motels around Copenhagen, or you can stay at a nearby village
kro (**country inn**). These usually small, former stagecoach inns
combine good personal service with wholesome food. **Board-
ing houses** *(pensionat)* and **private rooms** can be booked
through the Accommodation Bureau.

You will find that a hearty Danish breakfast is usually included in overnight rates, except at the most expensive hotels.

AIRPORT *(lufthavn)*

Copenhagen Airport, around 10 km (6 miles) from the city centre, is one of Europe's busiest. It is also a major gateway to Europe for travellers from the U.S.A., Canada, Japan, Australia,
and many countries in the Far East and Africa. About 40 airlines
have regular flights to and from Copenhagen. Danish domestic

flights also link up with destinations in Jutland, as well as with Funen and Bornholm islands, and various domestic flight concessions are made for foreign visitors.

Buses run from the airport every 15 minutes to the main railway station in central Copenhagen, a half hour's journey away. Others go to the port of Dragør (south of the airport) for the ferry connection to Limhamn in southern Sweden. A third bus service leaves for the downtown hydrofoil crossing to Malmö. Note that there is a new 10-minute rapid-transit train under construction, which will connect Copenhagen Airport with downtown Copenhagen.

Copenhagen Airport provides a good shopping centre, with duty-free self-service stores and a variety of boutiques and gift and souvenir shops, including souvenirs from Greenland. There's a bank, post office, nursery, a barber's shop and ladies' hairdresser, shower rooms, rest centre, Danish food shops, restaurant, and a large snack bar area—last chance for a *smørrebrød* and *wienerbrød* feast.

Porters and luggage trolleys are available. Taxis abound (for fares, see page 127). For **airport information,** ring 32 54 17 01.

Where's the bus for …?   **Hvorfra afgår bussen til …?**

B

BABYSITTERS

Hotel receptionists or the nearest tourist office are likely to know of local babysitting services; otherwise you could try the **Students** babysitting service (tel. 70 20 44 16); hours are Thursday noon to 6pm, other weekdays 10am to 3am; closed on Saturday and Sunday.

Can you get me a baby-sitter   **Kan De skaffe mig en**
tonight?   **babysitter til i for aften?**

BICYCLE HIRE *(cykeludlejning)*

Tourist offices will refer you to local dealers, or, in Copenhagen, you can go direct to **Københavns Cykelbørs** cycle-hire depot at Gothersgade 157, 1123 Copenhagen K (tel. 33 14 07 17). From April to October cycles can also be hired at many railway stations—nearest to Copenhagen are Klampenborg, Lyngby, Hillerød, and Helsingør—but advance booking is necessary, so call Central Station at 33 33 86 13. You can return the bike to another railway station in the country, if you prefer, on payment of a nominal freight charge. Organized cycling tours can be arranged through tourist offices in your country or tour operators in Denmark. Routes cover about 40–50 km (25–30 miles) a day, and you can choose to stay in a youth hostel, *kro* (inn), or hotel. See the *Cycling Holidays in Denmark* leaflet obtainable free from the **Danish Cyclist Federation,** Romersgade 7, DK-1362 Copenhagen K (tel. 33 32 31 21) and the Danish Tourist Board. Evidence of identity is always needed when hiring cycles. (**NB:** bicycles travel free as "personal luggage" if you bring your own from home.)

BUDGETING FOR YOUR TRIP

The following are some average prices in Danish kroner (kr) for basic expenses. However, remember that all prices must be regarded as *approximate*. Danes round off the bill, up or down, to the closest amount possible divisible by 25 øre because there are no intermediate coins (e.g., 13 is rounded off to 25).

Airport transfer. Bus to Rådhuspladsen 20kr. Special airport bus directly to Central Station 35kr; taxi 140kr (tip included).

Babysitters. 25kr per hour. Booking fee is 25kr, which includes transport.

Bicycle hire. 50kr a day, 225kr a week, deposit 200kr.

Camping. Camping pass for foreign visitors 30kr per person per night, children half price. Families 60kr.

Car hire. *Ford Escort 1.3* 920kr per day, 3,070kr per week; *Volvo 740* (station wagon) 1,350kr per day, 5,630kr per week; *Audi 100* (automatic) 1,135kr per day, 4,190kr per week; all prices include unlimited mileage, but exclude insurance. Add 25% tax.

Copenhagen

Copenhagen Card. One day 140kr, two days 255kr, three days 320kr. Half price for children under 12.

Entertainment. Cinema 40–65kr, Royal Ballet tickets 50–325kr, nightclub entry 30–60kr. Tivoli: adults 38kr, children half price.

Hotels. Top class 1,200–2,400kr, medium 700–900kr, inexpensive 500–700kr for double room with bathroom and breakfast.

Meals and drinks (at a fairly good establishment). Lunch 70kr, dinner 150kr, sandwich (*smørrebrød*) 15–20kr, coffee 12kr, akvavit (*schnaps*) 25kr, beer 25kr, soft drink 15kr.

Public transport. Flat-rate ticket (*grundbillet*) for single bus ride or S-train ride 11kr. Ticket coupons (*rabatkort*) for 10 rides: blue 70kr, yellow 100kr, lilac 165kr, grey 230kr.

Shopping bag. Bread 12kr, 250g of butter 10kr, 6 eggs 10kr, ½kg of beefsteak (choice meat) 50kr, 500g of instant coffee 50kr, bottle of beer 6kr, soft drink 5kr.

Taxi. Meter charge 22kr; 7kr per km between 6am and 6pm, 10kr per km between 6pm and 6am and at weekends.

C

CAMPING *(camping)*

More than 400 camping sites, seven of them less than 16 km (10 miles) from the centre of Copenhagen, are approved by the Camping Council, which means they are frequently visited by health and camping inspectors. The sites range from one- to three-star categories and cover basics from drinking water to provision stores and the services of camp wardens. Unless you have an *International Camping Carnet* you must obtain a Camping Pass for foreigners, valid for the rest of the year, at the first site visited. Camping on private land requires the owner's permission.

You can pick up an excellent free brochure on camping, youth hostels, and student hotels from the Danish Tourist Board in your country (see page 125 for addresses). Alternatively, for general information on camping in Denmark, contact Camping-grådet, Hesseløgade 16, 2100 Copenhagen Ø; tel. 39 27 88 44.

CAR HIRE *(biludlejning)* (See also DRIVING and BUDGETING FOR YOUR TRIP)

There are several car-hire counters at Copenhagen Airport, and the major international agencies are represented in the capital. Tourist information bureaux have lists of local firms. Otherwise, look up under *Autoudlejning* in the trade telephone directory *(Fagbog)*.

To hire a car, you'll need a valid national (or international) driving licence and be at least 21 years of age (25 for some firms). It's a good idea to have your passport available, too, although don't leave it with the company. Most agencies will require a cash deposit covering the estimated rental charge; as prices vary considerably, it's worth shopping around. Credit cards are accepted.

CLIMATE and CLOTHING

Climate. Denmark's relatively temperate climate is due to its situation and the sea currents, but frequent switches in the wind also bring changeable weather. Spring may come late, but summer is often sunny and autumn mild. Average monthly temperatures in Copenhagen are:

	J	F	M	A	M	J	J	A	S	O	N	D
temperature °C	0.5	0	2	6	11	16	17	16	13	9	5	2
temperature °F	33	32	35	42	52	60	63	61	56	48	40	36

Clothing. Casual clothes will fit nearly every occasion, including theatre and most dining out. Only in top-class hotels and clubs will men be required to wear a tie in the evening, and here women will not look out of place in something dressy. Otherwise, go as you like.

Summer nights are long and light but often chilly, so a sweater or cardigan is essential. Bring a light overcoat or raincoat too, in addition to ordinary summer clothes—the weather has an awkward habit of changing. On the beach, you can be as brief as you like.

Spring and autumn have many hours of sunshine, but winter can be downright cold and you should pack plenty of warm clothes (plus a raincoat). In all seasons, comfortable walking shoes are much to be recommended for your tours around the cobbled Old Town area.

COMMUNICATIONS (See also OPENING HOURS and TIME DIFFERENCES)

Post offices (*postkontor*). The main post office is at Tietgensgade 37, DK-1704 KBH (just behind Tivoli); business hours are Mon–Fri 10am–6pm, Saturday 9am–12pm, closed Sunday. The post office at the Central Station operates longer hours: Mon–Fri 8am–10pm, Saturday 9am–4pm, Sunday 10am–4pm. There are also many sub-offices around town. You cannot telephone post offices in Copenhagen, but enquiries can be made to the postal information service at 33 33 89 00. All post offices display a red sign with a crown, bugle, and crossed arrows in yellow — and a sign saying *Kongelig Post og Telegraf*. Stamp machines usually take two 1-kroner pieces. When buying postcards from stands and souvenir shops, you can get the appropriate stamps on the spot. Danish postboxes, bright red, stand out cheerfully, as do the postmen — colourful characters in red uniforms riding yellow cycles. You can pick up your **poste restante** (general-delivery) mail at the main post office at Tietgensgade 35-9 (postal address: 1500 Copenhagen V) from 11am to 6pm, Monday to Friday, and Saturday from 9am to 1pm, but not on Sunday. Identification is necessary.

Faxes and telex. Most hotels have fax and telex facilities. All post offices handle telegrams; call 122 (168 for information), or go to the nearest Telecom Centre.

Telephone (*telefon*). Apart from public telephones in newspaper and tobacco kiosks, public boxes are green-painted glass affairs with the word *telefon* on top. Insert 1 kroner for short local calls and 5 kroner for long-distance calls. Some telephone booths require the use of a card (a *Telet*), obtainable from kiosks all over town. Note that major North American calling cards can be used in Denmark.

For long-distance calls within Denmark, there are no area codes; just dial the 8-digit number of the person you want to call. Beware—telephoning from your hotel room can prove expensive.

Some useful numbers:

Telephone operation enquiries:	**141**
Directory enquiries:	**118**
International directory enquiries:	**113**
Directory-assisted international calls:	**115**
Telegram information:	**122**

A stamp for this letter/postcard, please.	**Et frimærke til dette brev/postkort, tak.**

CRIME (See also Emergencies and Police)

If Copenhagen still counts among the safest capital cities to walk around, things are not all they used to be. Pickpockets are rampant, and petty crime is on the increase. Take normal precautions. Keep a close eye on your belongings. Hesitate before walking out alone in the very early hours through seedy areas—your hotel receptionist can give advice if in doubt about night-time locations you wish to visit. It is best to avoid the Christiania area day and night.

CUSTOMS and ENTRY FORMALITIES (*toldkontrol*)

Most visitors—including citizens of the U.K., U.S.A., Canada, Ireland, Australia, and New Zealand—need only to possess a valid passport in order to enter Denmark. British subjects can enter on the simplified Visitor's Passport. You are generally entitled to stay in Denmark for up to three months without a visa. (This period includes the total amount of time spent in Denmark, Finland, Iceland, Norway, and Sweden in any six-month period.)

Copenhagen

As Denmark belongs to the **European Union (EU)**, free exchange of non-duty-free goods for personal use is permitted between Denmark and the U.K. and Ireland. However, duty-free items are still subject to restrictions: check before you go.

For residents of **non-EU** countries, restrictions are as follows: **Australia:** 250 cigarettes **or** 250g tobacco; 1l alcohol; **Canada:** 200 cigarettes **and** 50 cigars **and** 400g tobacco; 1.1l spirits **or** wine **or** 8.5l beer; **New Zealand:** 200 cigarettes **or** 50 cigars **or** 250g tobacco; 4.5l wine **or** beer **and** 1.1l spirits; **South Africa:** 400 cigarettes **and** 50 cigars **and** 250g tobacco; 2l wine **and** 1l spirits; **U.S.A.:** 200 cigarettes **and** 100 cigars **or** a "reasonable amount" of tobacco.

Currency restrictions. There is no limit on the amount of Danish or foreign currency that can be brought into or taken out of the country by non-residents. However, anything over 50,000kr can be exported only if it does not exceed the amount originally imported.

D

DISABLED TRAVELLERS

Many institutions in Denmark, as well as the government, pay particular attention to the needs of the disabled. The guide book *Access in Denmark—A Travel Guide for the Disabled* can be obtained from offices of the Danish Tourist Board (see page 125 for addresses). It gives a comprehensive list of accessible areas and facilities for wheelchair users, including public transport, museums, and accommodation.

The *Danish Hotel Guide* identifies hotels that are accessible to handicapped persons. For additional information, contact Disabled People's User Service, Kloverprisvej 10B, DK-2650 Hvidovre, Copenhagen, tel. 36 75 17 93. They provide information on approved campgrounds with facilities for the handicapped. Hostelling International Denmark, Vesterbrogade 39, DK-1620

Copenhagen V, tel. 31 31 36 12, designates hostels with facilities for the handicapped.

DRIVING (See also CAR HIRE)

To take your car into Denmark, you'll need:

- a valid driving licence, showing which type of vehicle it covers
- car registration papers
- Green Card (an extension of your regular insurance policy, valid for travel abroad; though not obligatory for EU countries, it's still preferable to have it)
- a red warning triangle in case of breakdown
- a national identity sticker for your car.

Driving conditions. Drive on the right, pass on the left. Traditionally, traffic coming from your right has priority, but this is decreasingly relevant in Denmark, where most junctions are clearly marked with white broken triangles (called "sharks' teeth" in Danish), halt signs, traffic lights, etc. Danish national policy is to abolish roundabouts, now considered dangerous because of priority confusion. The Danes are, on the whole, well disciplined drivers and they will expect you to be the same. Clear indication should always be given when changing lanes, either on motorways (expressways) or on the broad thoroughfares that cut through central Copenhagen. Weaving from one lane to another is a punishable offence.

Pedestrian crossings are sacrosanct and nearly always controlled by lights. When turning at lights, you *must* allow pedestrians on the road you are joining to cross first; equally, bikes have priority at any crossing if they want to go straight on when the car turns right.

Beware of buses pulling out from stops—you should give way to them. Caution, also, for cyclists and moped riders to your right, often on their own raised pathways (*cykelsti*), but sometimes divided from you merely by a white line, which you should not cross.

Copenhagen

Seat belts must be worn by driver and passengers. Motorcycle, moped, and scooter drivers, and their passengers, must wear helmets. British car-owners note: left dipping headlights are illegal.

Speed limits. On the *motorvej* (motorway/expressway), the limit is 100 km/h (68 mph). On other roads it is 80 km/h (50 mph) and in built-up areas—indicated by white signs with town silhouettes—it drops to 50 km/h (30 mph). Cars with caravans (trailers) may not exceed 70 km/h (44 mph). If you are caught speeding, there's a heavy fine—on the spot.

Parking. Traffic wardens in grey uniforms (and police) look for motorists who have parked near signs reading *stopforbudt* (no stopping) or *parkering forbudt* (no parking). They may only put a warning card on your windscreen, but they just might leave a ticket that'll mean a hefty fine. A car that causes a serious obstruction or is double-parked may well be towed away and impounded—and you'll have to pay for the towing, plus a fine. To judge whether you have parked longer than allowed, the warden will look at a disc you should display on your windscreen, indicating the time you arrived. These parking discs (*P-skive* or *parkeringsskive*) can be obtained free from police stations, garages, post offices, and most banks.

Stopping and waiting are not allowed within 5 metres (16 feet) of crossroads, pedestrian crossings, or exits from cycle tracks. Copenhagen's system of *Datostop* and *Dato-parkering* means that stopping or parking are allowed only on one side of the street—the side of the street with even numbers on even days, the side with odd numbers on odd days. For parking meters you will need 5-, 10-, and 20-kroner coins. Parked cars should by law always be left locked.

Drinking and driving. The penalties are severe: if you are discovered to have more than 0.8 millilitres of alcohol in your blood while driving, you face a fine equivalent to a month's wages, lose your licence for a year, and can be sent to a "lenient prison."

Breakdown. If you have a breakdown, you can call FALCK Rescue Service, the breakdown and towing service, in Copenhagen at 44 92 22 22 day and night. Road assistance (only) is given free of charge to members of FIA or AIT motoring organizations. If you aren't a member, you should take out an insurance policy in your home country. Note that a *MOMS* (VAT/sales tax) of 25% is added to all repair bills.

Fuel and oil (*benzin*; *olie*). Service stations are plentiful, and most international brands of fuel are available, but expensive. However, you can save a few øre per litre at a self-service station (variously called *selvbetjening, tank selv,* or "self-service").

Fluid measures

Road signs. International pictographs are in widespread use in Copenhagen, but below are translations of some written signs you may encounter:

Blind vej	Dead-end road (cul-de-sac)
Fare	Danger
Fodgængere	Pedestrians
Indkørsel forbudt	No entry
Omkørsel	Diversion
Rabatten er blød	Soft shoulders
Udkørsel	Exit
Vejarbejde	Roadworks

Copenhagen

Other useful vocabulary:

driving licence	**førerbevis**
car registration papers	**registreringsattest**
green card	**grønt kort**
Can I park here?	**Må jeg parkere her?**
Fill the tank, please …	**Vær venlig at fylde op med**
normal/super/unleaded	**almindelig/super/blyfri**
Check the oil/tyres/battery, please.	**Vær venlig at kontrollere olien/dækkene/batteriet.**
I've had a breakdown.	**Vognen er gået i stykker.**
There's been an accident.	**Der er sket en ulykke.**

E

ELECTRIC CURRENT

The standard voltage is 220, but some camping sites also have 110 available. Note that plugs and sockets in Denmark are different from both British and American types, but if you ask the hotel receptionist you should be able to find an adapter that you can use.

EMBASSIES and CONSULATES *(ambassade; konsulat)*

Australia: (consulate) Strandboulevarden, 2100 Copenhagen Ø; tel. 39 29 20 77

Canada: (embassy) Kristen Bernikowsgade 1, 1105 Copenhagen K; tel. 33 12 22 99

Ireland: (embassy) Østbanegade 21, 2100 Copenhagen Ø; tel. 31 42 32 33

South Africa: (consulate) Gammel Vartovvej 8, 2900 Hellerup; tel. 39 18 01 55

United Kingdom: (embassy and consulate) Kastelsvej 40, 2100 Copenhagen Ø; tel. 35 44 52 00

| U.S.A.: | (embassy and consulate) Dag Hammarskjölds Allé 24, 2100 Copenhagen Ø; tel. 35 55 31 44 |

EMERGENCIES (See also MEDICAL CARE and POLICE)

The all-purpose emergency number is **112,** and is free from public phone boxes. Ask for police, fire, or ambulance. Speak distinctly (English will be understood) and state your number and location.

Emergency service (*skadestue*) in central Copenhagen — for accidents only, 24 hours: Kommunehospitalet, Øster Farimagsgade 5, and Rigshospitalet, Blegdamsvej 9 and Tagensvej 20. Medical emergencies in Copenhagen, ring 32 84 00 41 or 33 93 63 00 8am–4pm daily and 24 hours at weekends.

Dental emergency. Tandlægevagten, Oslo Plads 14, is open year round, 8am–9:30pm weekdays; on Saturdays, Sundays and public holidays also 10am to noon, tel. 35 38 02 51. Cash payment only.

ETIQUETTE

The Danes are the most easily approachable as well as the least formal of all Scandinavians, but a handshake on meeting and departure is recognized practice. A pleasantly affable *goddag* ("good day" — pronounced almost as in English) is much appreciated, as is *farvel* ("farewell" or "goodbye," pronounced far-VELL).

G

GAY and LESBIAN TRAVELLERS

Denmark has one of Europe's most liberal attitudes towards gays and lesbians, and this is reflected in its legislation. In common with most of Scandinavia, the age of consent is the same as for heterosexuals. Copenhagen has a thriving gay scene, and there are bars, clubs, and a few hotels where gays are welcome. For information, contact the Landsforeningen for Bøsser og Lesbiske (National Organization for Gay Men and Women), Teglgårdstræde 13; tel. 33 13 19 48.

Copenhagen

GUIDES and TOURS *(guide)*

Sightseeing tour buses and some canal boats will be accompanied by a multilingual guide. Contact the tourist office at 33 11 13 25 for details of authorized guides, or consult the listings in *Copenhagen This Week*. Your hotel will also have information on tour programmes.

Brewery visits. A brewery tour is an excellent way to spend time, not only to sample a free bottle or two, but also to discover how every glass you drink is a contribution to art, science, or industry: Carlsberg and Tuborg donate vast sums through their charitable foundations. **Carlsberg** (tel. 33 27 13 14) is at the Elephant Gate, Ny Carlsbergvej 140 (bus 6 from Rådhuspladsen); guided tours in several languages at 11am and 2pm.

Canal and harbour tours. Though the city hasn't as extensive a network of waterways as Venice or Amsterdam, Copenhagen's canals offer a delightful 50-minute trip on a fine day. Gammel Strand and Nyhavn (at Kongens Nytorv) are the two main starting points. From May to October, 90-minute waterbus tours— some with guided commentary—give you an excellent view of the inner city and harbour.

City tours. Copenhagen Excursions and Vikingbus operate organized **bus tours** covering the major sights; duration from 1½ to 2¾ hours. The **Royal Tour** includes a visit to the Reception Chambers at Christiansborg Palace and the crown jewels at Rosenborg, while the **Grand Tour** aims to give visitors an overall impression of the city, ending with attendance at the changing of the guard ceremony at Amalienborg Palace. There are also guided **walking tours** of Copenhagen several times weekly during the summer, with an English-speaking guide. Guided **tours by bike** operate between June and October. Other tours run by taxi, limousine, and sightseeing flights.

Industrial art tours. There are guided tours in English of the Royal Copenhagen **porcelain** factory, Smallegade 45, between

June and September Monday to Friday at 9am, 10am, and 11am, also at 1pm and 2pm in the summer. Similar tours run to **silver** and **glass** works.

Themed tours. Choose between a leisurely afternoon **Hamlet** tour or a full day's trip to North Zealand's **castles.** Also a 6-hour **Vikingland** tour (Roskilde cathedral and the Viking Ship Museum), an 11-hour trip to **Hans Christian Andersen**'s home town of Odense on the island of Funen, and a 13-hour tour to **Legoland** (advance booking essential).

Trips to Sweden. Sweden is so close and accessible that it really is worth the short trip—if only to see how Swedes differ from Danes.

From Havnegade, Nyhavn, in the centre of Copenhagen, two companies—Flyvebådene and Pilen—offer a 45-minute catamaran service right into the heart of Malmö. An alternative is to combine a trip to Helsingør with the 20-minute ferryboat service to Helsingborg.

The more adventurous can try a "Round the Sound" trip. Buy your tickets from DBS (Danish State Railways) and travel, in either direction, from Copenhagen to Malmö, up to Helsingborg by train, across the sound to Helsingør, and back to Copenhagen by train.

L

LANGUAGE

English is very widely spoken and understood. Danish is perhaps the most difficult northern-European language for relating the written word to speech; it's almost impossible to pronounce simply by reading the words, as many syllables are swallowed rather than spoken. Thus the island of Amager becomes *Am-air,* with the "g" disappearing, but in a distinctive Danish way difficult for the visitor to imitate. The letter "d" becomes something like a "th," but with the tongue placed behind the lower teeth, not the upper. The letter "ø" is like the

Copenhagen

"u" in English n**u**rse, but spoken with the lips far forward. And the letter "r" is again swallowed.

There are 29 letters in the Danish alphabet—the 26 "normal," plus "æ" (as in **e**gg), "ø," and "å" (as in p**o**rt). They appear *after* the usual 26 (a point to note when looking up names in phone books and lists).

Days

Monday	**mandag**	Friday	**fredag**
Tuesday	**tirsdag**	Saturday	**lørdag**
Wednesday	**onsdag**	Sunday	**søndag**
Thursday	**torsdag**		

Months

January	**januar**	July	**juli**
February	**februar**	August	**august**
March	**marts**	September	**september**
April	**april**	October	**oktober**
May	**maj**	November	**november**
June	**juni**	December	**december**

Numbers

0	**nul**	10	**ti**	20	**tyve**
1	**en**	11	**elleve**	30	**tredive**
2	**to**	12	**tolv**	40	**fyrre**
3	**tre**	13	**tretten**	50	**halvtreds**
4	**fire**	14	**fjorten**	60	**tres**
5	**fem**	15	**femten**	70	**halvfjerds**
6	**seks**	16	**seksten**	80	**firs**
7	**syv**	17	**sytten**	90	**halvfems**
8	**otte**	18	**atten**	100	**hundrede**
9	**ni**	19	**nitten**	1000	**tusind**

LAUNDRY and DRY CLEANING *(vask; kemisk rensning)*

The large hotels offer same-day service, but not on weekends and holidays—and it's expensive. Dry cleaners are found throughout the city and are entered in the directory *(Fagbog)* under *Renserier*. Prices in launderettes *(selvbetjeningsvaskeri)* are lower, and these are open till late at night.

When will it be ready?	**Hvornår er det færdigt?**
I must have this for tomorrow morning.	**Jeg skal bruge det i morgen tidlig.**

LOST PROPERTY *(hittegods)*

The **general** lost-property office *(hittegodskontor)* is at the police station at Slotsherrensvej 113, Vanløse (tel. 38 74 52 61), Mon–Thurs 9am–5:30pm, Friday 9am–2pm, closed Saturday and Sunday. For property lost in **buses** or **trains,** the address to contact is Lyshøjgårdsvej 80, Valby; for buses tel. 36 45 45 45, open daily 7am–9:30pm; for trains tel. 31 16 21 10 Mon–Fri 9am–4pm. For missing **credit cards** call Eurocard Denmark, tel. 44 89 25 00 (24 hours) or, for American Express cardholders, tel. 80 01 00 21.

M

MEDIA

Newspapers and magazines *(avis; ugeblad)*. You'll have no problem finding English-language newspapers and magazines at newsstands, shops, and hotels throughout central Copenhagen. The kiosk at the Central Station sells foreign-language publications, and you'll find a good selection at Magasin du Nord (Kongens Nytorv 13) and Illums (52-54 Østergade) department stores. There is also a free monthly English-language brochure, *Copenhagen This Week*, which lists comprehensive information for visitors.

Copenhagen

Radio and TV (*radio; fjernsyn*). Danish radio has three channels—Radio 1 (on 90.8 MHz VHF) for news and comment and classical music, and channels 2 and 3 (96.5/93.9 MHz) for local news, lighter music, and entertainment. There's a news programme in English on Radio 3 (93.8 MHz) at 8:30am Monday to Friday. BBC long-wave and world services and European-based American networks can be picked up.

The main television transmission is from 7:30am to 11:30pm. All films are shown in their original version with Danish subtitles.

Have you any English-language newspapers?	**Har De engelsksprogede aviser?**

MEDICAL CARE (See also EMERGENCIES)

Make sure your health insurance covers any illness or accident while on holiday. Your travel agent or insurance company will advise you.

In Denmark, treatment and even hospitalization is free for any tourist taken suddenly ill or involved in an accident. For minor treatments, doctors, dentists, and chemists (druggists) will charge on the spot. For EU employees or pensioners and their families, however, this money will be partly refunded at the local Danish health service office on production of bills and the EU form E111. It's wise to ask before you go about possible reciprocal health agreements and any forms needed.

A Danish **chemist/pharmacy** (*apotek*) is strictly a dispensary. Some medicines which can be bought over the counter in other countries are available only on prescription. Pharmacies are listed in the trade phone book under *Apoteker*. Normal hours are from 9am to 5:30pm and until 1pm on Saturday. An all-night service operates at Steno Apotek, Vesterbrogade 6C, tel. 33 14 82 66; and at Sonderbro Apotek, Amangerbrog. 158, tel. 31 58 01 40.

I need a doctor/dentist. **Jeg har brug for en
læge/tandlæge.**

MONEY MATTERS (See also CUSTOMS AND ENTRY FORMALITIES)

Currency. The unit of Danish currency is the *kroner*, abbreviated *kr*, or, abroad, Dkr (to distinguish it from the Norwegian and Swedish kroner). It is divided into 100 *øre*.

Coins: 25 and 50 *øre*; 1, 2, 5, 10, and 20 *kroner.*

Banknotes: 50, 100, 500, and 1,000 *kroner.*

Banks and currency-exchange offices (*bank; vekselkontor*). Banks and bureaux de change offer the best exchange rates for foreign cash. You pay a flat commission per transaction at banks, which are open Mon–Fri 9:30am–4pm (6pm on Thursday). Outside banking hours, exchange bureaux operate at the Central Station every day of the week from 6:45am to 10pm and at the entrance to Tivoli in H.C. Andersens Boulevard from noon to 11pm during the high season (May to mid-September). Exchange bureaux also sell Copenhagen Cards, stamps, and bus and train tickets.

Credit cards and traveller's cheques (*kreditkort; rejsecheck*). Major hotels and many restaurants—and some tourist shops, too—will accept payment by international credit cards. There's little problem with traveller's cheques, provided you bring along passport identification. Both traveller's cheques and Eurocheques can also be cashed at banks in Denmark.

MOMS. Danish VAT (sales tax) is called *MOMS* and is set at 25%. It's always included in the bill. For expensive purchases (over 600kr), there are special tax-free export schemes. Look out for shops displaying the signs Europe Tax-Free Shopping or Tax-Free International; retailers are well acquainted with the necessary procedures.

OPENING HOURS

Banks are open Monday–Friday 9:30am–4pm, Thursday until 6pm. In the provinces, hours fluctuate from town to town.

Post offices are open 9 or 10am–5 or 5:30pm during the week; some post offices also open on Saturday 9am–noon.

Shops and **department stores** are generally open Monday–Friday 9:30 or 10am–5:30pm; recently Danish shopping hours have been officially extended, permitting shops to be open from 6am to 8pm if they elect to do so. Some are closed on Monday or Tuesday. Shops are usually open from 9am to 1 or 2pm on Saturday.

There are no regularized hours for **museums** in Copenhagen, and times are subject to frequent change. The most likely closing day is Monday, and shorter hours generally operate during the winter.

P

PHOTOGRAPHY

Film is relatively inexpensive, so it's not worth bringing a stock from home. Developing and printing are of a high quality and can be done quickly in the centre; try **Express Foto,** Amargerbrogade 101, tel. 31 55 27 37.

I'd like a film for this camera.	**Jeg vil gerne have en film til dette apparat.**
a black-and-white film	**en sort-hvid film**
colour prints	**en farvefilm**
colour slides	**en film til lysbilleder**
How long will it take to develop (and print) this film?	**Hvor lang tid tager det at fremkalde (og kopiere) denne film?**
May I take a picture?	**Må jeg tage et billede?**

POLICE (See also EMERGENCIES)

State and city police all form part of the national force and are dressed in black uniforms. Some walk their beat through central Copenhagen, but most policemen patrol in deep-blue-and-white or white cars with the word *POLITI* in large letters (although they also tend to roam around in unmarked cars). You're entitled to stop police cars at any time and request help. Police are courteous and speak English (they take a mandatory 80 English lessons during training).

Don't hesitate to go to the local police station if in need of advice. All are listed in the phone book under *Politi*.

Where's the nearest police station?	**Hvor er den nærmeste politi-station?**

PUBLIC HOLIDAYS (*fest-/helligdag*)

Though Denmark's banks, offices, and major shops close on public holidays, museums and tourist attractions will be open, if perhaps on reduced hours. Everything will also be business as usual in the cafés.

1 January	*Nytår*	New Year's Day
5 June (half-day)	*Grundslovsdag*	Constitution Day
25/26 December	*Jul*	Christmas
Movable dates:	*Skærtorsdag*	Maundy Thursday
	Langfredag	Good Friday
	Anden påskedag	Easter Monday
	Bededag	General Prayer Day (fourth Friday after Easter)
	Kristi himmelfartsdag	Ascension Day
	Anden pinsedag	Whit Monday

Are you open tomorrow?	**Har De åbent i morgen?**

R

RELIGIOUS SERVICES

The Danish Church is Protestant (Evangelical Lutheran). Sunday services in English are held in the following places of worship:

Church of England. St. Alban's Anglican Episcopalian Church, Churchillparken, Langelinie. Morning services, Holy Communion. Tel. 39 62 77 36.

The American Church of Copenhagen. Interdenominational and international, Farvergade 27. Services every Sunday morning, followed by Coffee Fellowship. Tel. 39 62 47 85.

Roman Catholic. Jesu Hjerte Kirke, Stenosgade 4. Morning mass. Tel. 31 21 85 88.

Jewish services are held in Hebrew in the Synagogue, Krystalgade 12, daily in the early morning and evening. Tel. 33 12 88 68.

T

TIME DIFFERENCES

Denmark sticks to Central European Time (GMT + 1) along with most of the Continent. In summer, the clock is put one hour ahead (GMT + 2), and the time differences look like this:

New York	London	**Copenhagen**	Jo'burg	Sydney	Auckland
7am	noon	**1pm**	1pm	9pm	11pm

What time is it, please?　　　　**Undskyld, hvad er klokken?**

TIPPING

This is a non-existent problem since basically you don't give tips. Hotel and restaurant bills always include service; tip only if special services have been rendered. Railway porters charge fixed prices, and no need to tip hairdressers, taxi drivers, or theatre or cinema ushers. Only in a very few cases is there an exception to the rule, as, for instance, when you leave the odd kroner tip for use of the washbasin and facilities in toilets.

TOILETS/RESTROOMS

Facilities are usually indicated by a pictograph; alternatively they are marked *WC*, *Toiletter*, *Damer/Herrer* (Ladies/Gentlemen), or just by *D/H*. There's no charge unless you see it clearly marked otherwise.

Where are the toilets?   **Hvor er toilettet?**

TOURIST INFORMATION OFFICES *(turistinformation)*

Danish tourist offices are often very helpful, and can provide copious information and a range of first-class brochures.

United Kingdom: Danish Tourist Board, 55 Sloane Street, London SW1X 95Y; tel. (0171) 259 5959.

U.S.A.: Scandinavian National Tourist Offices, 655 Third Avenue, 18th floor, New York, NY 10017; tel. (212) 885-9700.

All Danish cities and most small towns have their own tourist information office marked by a large letter "**i**" on a green background. The main tourist information office is near Tivoli at Bernstorffsgade 1, DK-1577 Copenhagen, tel. 33 11 13 25, open daily 9am–8pm during the summer; winter Monday–Saturday 9am–5pm, closed Sunday.

Where's the tourist office?   **Hvor ligger turistbureauet?**

TRANSPORT

Bus and S-Train. An excellent public transport system of frequent buses (*bus*) and electrified trains (*S-tog*) starts weekdays at 5am and Sunday at 6am. The last main services leave the centre at 12:30am, although there are several all-night buses (*natbusser*). For bus information, call 36 45 45 45, then dial 3 for personal service (7am–11pm); for S-train information, tel. 33 14 17 01 (Central Station).

Tickets. The fare system in Copenhagen is somewhat complicated. It is valid for the HT-area—the city and surrounding region of 40 km (24 miles)—which has been split into zones. Tickets entitle you to travel and transfer within a zone and to bordering zones for a limited period of time. Tickets are interchangeable on buses and trains, which begin like an underground railway in the central district and then emerge into daylight on the suburban network.

Purchase a flat-fare ticket (*grundbillet*) for single rides within a zone and to bordering zones only. Additional tickets, available at an extra cost, are required if you travel beyond the basic ticket zone. The more advantageous ticket coupons (*rabatkort*) are valid for 10 rides in several zones. Blue coupons are good for 2 zones, yellow for 3 zones, lilac for 5 zones, and grey for all zones. They can be purchased at train stations or from bus drivers.

Enter by the front door, tell the driver your destination, and you'll be given the right ticket. Don't forget to time-stamp your coupon (face up) aboard the bus or in the yellow automatic machines on train platforms. Passengers without valid stamped tickets are liable to on-the-spot fines. Children under 7 travel free, ages 7 to 14 half-fare.

Car ferries. Since Denmark is largely an archipelago, it's hardly surprising that car ferries are a familiar feature of the country's everyday life. Though spectacular bridges have been built linking some of the islands, a good many places can still only be reached by boat. You certainly won't be disappointed in the regular, efficient ferry services that conveniently cover the islands and the Jutland peninsula. All the major routes carry both cars and passengers. Detailed timetables including rates and conditions are available from the Danish National Tourist Board, in English. Fares vary according to the weight and length of the car; prices quoted may include passengers, so check beforehand. It's highly advisable to book a day ahead, at least for domestic crossings—the Danes do, especially in summer when boats tend to be quite full. Be in good time (at least 30 minutes ahead) for embarkation, or you'll probably lose your reservation.

Taxi. Plenty of taxis cruise the streets of Copenhagen, but in wet weather it's difficult to find a vacant one. They are recognized by a *Taxi* or *Taxa* sign. Vacant cabs display the word *FRI* (free). Tips are included in the meter price, but round the sum off upwards—if pleased with service. All cabs are radio-controlled; call 31 35 35 35 or 32 51 51 51—or for a mini-bus taxi, 31 39 35 35. Most drivers speak English.

Copenhagen and its suburbs extend for miles, so before leaping into the nearest available cab, do have a look at where your destination lies and check on the availability of a cheaper bus or train service.

Trains (*tog*). A comprehensive and punctual network dealing with 1,200 movements a day operates from Copenhagen Central Station.

Regional or coast diesel trains (*Kystbanerne*) cover the outer Zealand area.

Intercity trains (*Intercity*) are the backbone of Danish State Railways' (*DSB-Danske Statsbaner*) long-distance traffic. For instance, one leaves every hour for Jutland; the whole train is shunted aboard the Great Belt ferry to Funen island (seat reservations are required for through-passengers; ring the Central Station at 33 14 17 01).

Long-distance trains (*Lyntog*), "ultra-specials" reaching 140 km/h (87 mph), also run to Jutland and, like Intercity trains, have buffet bars, plus phones for passengers' use (seat reservations are required).

International trains, usually referred to by name (e.g., *Vikingen* or *Øresundspilen* for Stockholm), link Copenhagen with most of Europe. They have sleeping cars and couchette coaches for night travel.

Copenhagen

Copenhagen Card. Similar to a plastic credit card, this discount tourist card offers unlimited travel on buses and trains in metropolitan Copenhagen, free entrance to many of the major museums and sights, and up to 50 percent discount on ferry routes connecting Zealand with Sweden and on hydrofoils between Copenhagen and Malmö. The card is valid for one (140kr), two (255kr), or three (320kr) days, offers children 3 to 11 a 50% discount, and is on sale at tourist information offices (see page 125 for addresses), travel agencies, currency-exchange bureaus, all main railway stations in Denmark, and at certain Copenhagen hotels.

TRAVELLING TO COPENHAGEN (See also AIRPORT)

If the choice of ways to go is bewildering, the complexity of fares and regulations can be downright stupefying. A reliable travel agent will have full details of all the latest flights, fares, and regulations.

By Air. Copenhagen Airport is on several intercontinental routes — mainly from North America and the Middle and Far East. There are frequent regional services from most European cities. Average journey time London–Copenhagen is 1 hour and 45 minutes, New York–Copenhagen 7 hours and 40 minutes. From the U.K. an alternative service is run by AIR U.K. from the less-congested Stansted airport, accessible from Liverpool Street Station via the Stansted Express.

By Rail/Sea/Car. Ferry services to Denmark are generally into Esbjerg (from the U.K.), to Gedser (from Germany), and to numerous ports (including Copenhagen itself) for travellers arriving from Norway and Sweden.

Inter-Rail and *Eurail* cards are valid on all routes into Denmark.

There are road and rail links into Jutland from Schleswig-Holstein in Germany, and also through-trains from Hamburg to Copenhagen.

A new bridge and tunnel connecting Copenhagen and Malmø, Sweden, is under construction. Called the Øresund Fixed Link, it is scheduled for completion in the year 2000.

W

WATER *(vand)*

You can drink water without any qualms from the tap in Denmark. Locally bottled mineral water, if you prefer it, is excellent.

A glass of water, please.　　　　　　　　**Et glas vand, tak.**

WEIGHTS and MEASURES

For fluid and distance measurements, see page 113. Denmark uses the metric system.

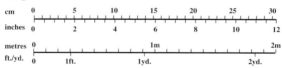

Length

| cm | 0 | 5 | 10 | 15 | 20 | 25 | 30 |
| inches | 0 | 2 | 4 | 6 | 8 | 10 | 12 |

| metres | 0 | | 1m | | 2m |
| ft./yd. | 0 | 1ft. | 1yd. | | 2yd. |

Weight

| grams | 0 | 100 | 200 | 300 | 400 | 500 | 600 | 700 | 800 | 900 | 1kg |
| ounces | 0 | 4 | 8 | 12 | 1lb | 20 | 24 | 28 | 2lb |

Temperature

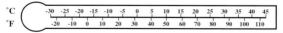

| °C | -30 | -25 | -20 | -15 | -10 | -5 | 0 | 5 | 10 | 15 | 20 | 25 | 30 | 35 | 40 | 45 |
| °F | -20 | -10 | 0 | 10 | 20 | 30 | 40 | 50 | 60 | 70 | 80 | 90 | 100 | 110 |

Copenhagen

WOMEN TRAVELLERS

Women can wander almost anywhere in Copenhagen without being subjected to sexual harassment. As in most cities around the world, however, it is prudent to avoid travelling alone late at night on the underground and to keep away from the "red light" area that centres around the railway station.

Y

YOUTH HOSTELS *(vandrerhjem)*

Copenhagen is something of a mecca for rucksack travellers. There are ten city youth hostels and student hotels to cater for the influx and to prevent sleeping rough in the parks, which is frowned upon. Youth hostels as such require a membership card issued by an organization affiliated to the International Youth Hostel Association. If you haven't got such a card, you can obtain a guest card from Denmark's Youth Hostels (address below).

Bed linen can be hired at the hostel (down bags are not permitted). There's no age limit. A full list of Denmark's 100-odd youth hostels is available on request from Danish Tourist Board offices abroad.

Danmarks Vandrerhjem (Denmark's Youth Hostels), Vesterbrogade 39, 1620 Copenhagen V; tel. 31 31 36 12. Open Mon–Thurs 9am–4pm, Friday until 3pm. April–August Thursday 9am–6pm.

At a student hotel (*ungdomsherberg*), restrictions on nighttime closure and other practises are more relaxed.

For any information specifically in the youth field, call in at **Huset** (*"Use It"*) downtown youth information centre (see page 26) at Rådhusstræde 13 (tel. 33 15 65 18), open Monday through Thursday 10am to 4pm, Friday 10am to 2pm. At other times a noticeboard indicates room availability.

Recommended Hotels

Copenhagen's hotels tend to be clustered around the centre. All are within a very short walking distance of the city's main sights—Rådhuspladsen, the lively shopping street Strøget, and the Tivoli Gardens. The main railway station is a mere 5 minutes walk away from the centre, while the airport lies a brief 20-minute journey away by car or bus.

We have listed the following Copenhagen establishments according to their different price categories. Prices are based on the cost per night of a double room with *en suite* bath or shower (unless indicated otherwise), including service charge, VAT *(MOMS)* and breakfast.

It is always advisable to reserve ahead of your stay. The city is at its busiest in the summer months (June to August), but conferences ensure that hotels are kept busy throughout the year.

We have included hotels within easy reach of the city, as well as some in more distant places that are suitable for excursions. Should you come across an establishment worth recommending, we would be pleased to hear from you.

✹	below 700kr
✹✹	700–1,200kr
✹✹✹	above 1,200kr

COPENHAGEN

Admiral Hotel ✹✹ *Tolbodgade 24-28, 1253 Copenhagen K; Tel. 33 11 82 82, fax 33 32 55 42.* Standing beside the harbour, the hotel was formerly a granary, built 200 years ago. Comfortably converted, it has retained the wooden beams in the rooms. With its own restaurant; sauna. 366 rooms.

Alexandra ✹✹ *H.C. Andersens Boulevard 8, 1553 Copenhagen V; Tel. 33 14 22 00, fax 33 14 02 84.* A lovely old hotel, pleasantly decorated, with light, airy rooms and excellent facilities (including underground parking). Although the hotel has no restaurant, the bar serves breakfast. 61 rooms.

Ascot ❀❀ *Studiestræde 61, 1554 Copenhagen V; Tel. 33 12 60 00, fax 33 14 60 40.* Set in a distinguished old building a few steps from City Hall, this hotel is pleasantly decorated with a mixture of antiques and modern furniture. There is no restaurant, but breakfast buffet and room service are both available. 150 rooms and suites, with a range of studios and penthouse apartments.

Astoria ❀ *Banegårdspladsen 4, 1570 Copenhagen V; Tel. 33 14 14 19, fax 33 14 08 02.* The Astoria dates from 1936, and is an excellent architectural example of Cubist style. It has been lovingly preserved, though the rooms have been updated to meet modern tastes. It is particularly suitable for families, and the recent introduction of bunk beds has proved a great success with both families and backpackers. The hotel serves a good breakfast buffet. It is recommended that guests book in advance. 94 rooms.

Centrum ❀ *Helgolandsgade 14, 1653 Copenhagen V; Tel. 31 31 31 11, fax 31 23 32 51.* An economy/tourist class hotel located in a quiet part of the city to the west of the centre. The building dates from the Victorian era, but the hotel has been fully modernized. Half the rooms have a private bathroom and colour TV. The budget rooms are without private facilities but guests will find modern bathrooms available on every floor. There is a bar and a restaurant that serves breakfast only (it is available, however, for groups if lunch and/or dinner has been ordered together with accommodation). 80 rooms.

Christian IV ❀ *Dronningens Tværgade 45, 1302 Copenhagen K; Tel. 33 32 10 44, fax 33 32 07 06.* Located almost on the doorstep of the lovely King's Garden, this is a small, airy hotel which is efficiently run. Rooms tend to be neat and bright, and are fitted out with modern Danish furniture. There is no restaurant on site, but breakfast is served in a pleasant dining room. 42 rooms.

City ✿ *Peder Skramsgade 24, 1054 Copenhagen K; Tel. 33 13 06 66, fax 33 13 06 67.* Set in an elegant town house, the City has a definite international feel to it, clearly expressed in the hotel's brand-new, striking modern décor. Personal service, however, remains high on the management's list of priorities, making for a hospitable, friendly atmosphere. Although the restaurant only serves breakfast, there is also a café on site. 81 rooms.

Comfort Hotel Excelsior ✿ *Colbjørnsensgade 6, 1652 Copenhagen V; Tel. 33 25 22 33, fax 33 24 50 87.* Located just west of the city centre, the hotel offers rooms with telephone, television, and mini-bar. 99 rooms and 1 apartment.

Cosmopole ✿ *Colbjørnsensgade 5-11, 1652 Copenhagen V; Tel. 33 21 33 33, fax 31 31 33 99.* A superior tourist-class hotel, furnished in a modern Scandinavian style, with simple, unpretentious décor and service. 208 rooms.

Danmark ✿ *Vester Voldgade 89, 1552 Copenhagen V; Tel. 33 11 48 06, fax 33 14 36 30.* A family-run hotel that is conveniently situated right in the heart of Copenhagen close to Strøget and Rådhuspladsen, in a modern, bright building. Rooms are tastefully furnished in subdued Scandinavian style, all with bathrooms and television. Only breakfast is served, though drinks are available throughout the day. Also underground parking and conference facilities. 51 rooms.

Grand Hotel ✿✿ *Vesterbrogade 9A, 1620 Copenhagen V; Tel. 31 31 36 00, fax 31 31 33 50.* This historic building has been carefully modernized in a manner that preserves much of its original character. Lovely rooms, tastefully decorated. Restaurant Oliver and Grand Bar. 146 rooms, 2 suites.

Hotel d'Angleterre ✿✿✿ *Kongens Nytorv 34, 1021 Copenhagen K; Tel. 33 12 00 95, fax 33 12 11 18.* One of the oldest deluxe hotels in the world, Hotel d'Angleterre was originally built in 1630, and reconstructed in 1755. This is one of those classic establishments where bathrooms are adorned with marble, gold-plated fittings, and snow-white towels. Inside there are two restaurants: Le Restaurant d'Angleterre, serving a menu of international food that is changed every few days; and Restaurant Wünblad, which offers more traditional Danish fare. A great favourite with business people, and much appreciated by the tourists as well. 130 rooms, including 18 suites.

Hotel Hebron ✿ *Helgolandsgade 4, 1653 Copenhagen V; Tel. 31 31 69 06, fax 31 31 90 67.* Quiet location close to the heart of the city, with its rooms benefiting from the soundproof double glazing installed throughout the hotel. Rooms are bright, spacious, and well equipped. Suitable for families. The hotel's restaurant serves breakfast only. 98 rooms.

Hotel Triton ✿✿ *Helgolandsgade 7-11, 1653 Copenhagen V; Tel. 31 31 32 66, fax 31 31 69 70.* A comfortable hotel located to the west of the centre. There is a bar, though no restaurant. 123 rooms.

Komfort ✿✿ *LØngangsstræde 27, 1468 Copenhagen V; Tel. 33 12 65 70, fax 33 15 28 99.* A welcoming modern hotel, with bright rooms, a lively English pub, and restaurant. Also underground parking. 202 rooms, including two quads and 7 triples.

Kong Arthur ✿ *NØrre SØgade 11, 1370 Copenhagen V; Tel. 33 11 12 12, fax 33 32 61 30.* Inaugurated in 1882, this hotel has retained much of its original charm. Situated beside Peblinge Lake. A family-run establishment, Kong Arthur is a popular choice with both Danish and foreign visitors; friendly and thoroughly Danish atmosphere. Pleasant breakfast room overlooks a pretty patio. Choice of restaurants. Good value. There are also sauna facilities and free parking. 107 rooms, 7 suites.

Le Sommelier ✿ *Bredgade 65, 1260 Copenhagen K; Tel. 33 11 45 15, fax 33 11 59 79.* Located along the once-fashionable stretch of Bredgade, this hotel has the atmosphere of an English bed and breakfast. Restaurant and bar. 90 rooms.

Mayfair ✹✹ *Helgolandsgade 3, 1650 Copenhagen V; Tel. 31 31 48 01, fax 31 23 96 86.* A turn-of-the-century hotel which has been recently refurbished, the Mayfair is privately owned, and offers a cosy atmosphere coupled with a very high standard of personal service. Its restaurant serves a large buffet-style breakfast. 101 rooms, plus 4 suites.

Neptun ✹✹✹ *Skt Annæ Plads 14-20, 1250 Copenhagen K; Tel. 33 13 89 00, fax 33 14 12 50.* Originally built in 1854, the hotel is decorated with beautiful Scandinavian antiques and contemporary paintings. Gourmet restaurant in cosy surroundings; attractive courtyard. 134 rooms.

Opera ✹✹ *Todenskjoldsgade 15, 1055 Copenhagen K; Tel. 33 12 15 19, fax 33 32 12 82.* A few steps away from the Royal Theatre. The building dates from 1869 and has recently undergone renovation, with "Olde England" décor now installed throughout. An excellent choice for families. 91 rooms.

Palace ✹✹✹ *Rådhuspladsen 57, 1550 Copenhagen V; Tel. 33 14 40 50, fax 33 14 52 79.* An imposing historical landmark located on the Town Hall Square, the Palace has been carefully renovated and modernized over the years so as to offer a high standard of accommodation, with spacious bedrooms and health club facilities. The hotel's one restaurant, Brasserie on the Square, serves a good selection of both international and Danish cuisine, while elsewhere there is a cocktail bar. 162 rooms, including 21 Ambassador rooms.

The Plaza ✹✹✹ *Bernstorffsgade 4, 1577 Copenhagen V; Tel. 33 14 92 62, fax 31 22 21 99.* A comfortable, well-equipped hotel, with beautifully appointed rooms and lovely decoration throughout. The attractive Library Bar, brimming with antique books and works of art, is a fine place to enjoy a drink, as well as being one of the most civilized rendezvous in Copenhagen. The Flora Danica restaurant offers Danish-style buffets. 93 rooms.

Copenhagen

Radisson SAS Royal ✹✹✹ *Hammerichsgade 1, 1611 Copenhagen; Tel. 33 14 14 12, fax 33 42 61 00.* Dating only from 1960, this modern hotel follows the best tradition of avant-garde Danish design. The Summit restaurant, situated on the 20th floor, offers a spectacular panoramic view of the city. Down in the lobby, the more informal Café Royal serves sandwiches and snacks. A haven for business people, it also attracts tourists during holidays, especially from June to August. Sauna. 265 rooms.

SAS Scandinavia ✹✹✹ *Amager Boulevard 70, 2300 Copenhagen S; Tel. 33 96 50 00, fax 31 96 55 00.* Another well-equipped hotel, with all the facilities and comfort you would expect of this internationally established chain. Indoor swimming pool, sauna. Largest hotel in the capital, with 542 rooms.

Scandic Hotel Copenhagen ✹✹✹ *Vester Søgade 6, PO Box 337, 1601 Copenhagen V; Tel. 33 14 35 35, fax 33 32 12 23.* Modern, 17-storey building, offering a whole range of facilities, including a health club and on-site parking. The Blue Garden restaurant serves both international and Danish cuisine, while the Café R offers light meals and snacks. In addition there are two bars: the Red Lion English pub and The Hours Bar. 435 rooms, 36 suites.

Selandia ✹ *Helgolandsgade 12, 1653 Copenhagen V; Tel 31 31 46 10, fax 31 31 46 09.* An unpretentious, functional hotel with comfortable rooms, most of which have private bath or shower. Friendly service. The hotel's restaurant serves breakfast only, but beverages are readily available throughout the day. 87 rooms.

71 Nyhavn Hotel ✹✹✹ *Nyhavn 71, 1051 Copenhagen K; Tel. 33 11 85 85, fax 33 93 15 85.* A former warehouse in a glorious setting on Copenhagen's waterfront, 71 Nyhavn Hotel is full of character. The rooms are small but many retain their wooden beams. Ask for a room with a view. The restaurant Pakhuskœlderen serves fine Danish cuisine, while Fyrskibet (an old restored Danish lightship anchored outside the hotel) is available for private functions. 82 rooms, including 6 suites.

Sophie Amalie Hotel ✻ *Sankt Annæ Plads 21, 1250 Copenhagen K; Tel. 33 13 34 00, fax 33 11 77 07.* Situated on the harbour front adjacent to Amalienborg Palace, this hotel was recently refurbished to provide good accommodation at a reasonable price. Lovely views of the new Copenhagen harbour promenade and the picturesque buildings surrounding Nyhavn and Amalienborg. 134 rooms.

Webers ✻✻ *Vesterbrogade 11B, 1620 Copenhagen V; Tel. 31 31 14 32, fax 31 31 14 41.* A modern building fitted out with reproduction antique furniture and also offering a lovely courtyard. The restaurant serves breakfast only, but there is also a bar. Health-club facilities. 160 rooms.

FARTHER AFIELD

Eremitage ✻✻✻ *Lyngby Storcenter 62, 2800 Lyngby; Tel. 45 88 77 00, fax 45 88 17 82.* A modern hotel, 10 km (6 miles) from central Copenhagen, and five minutes' walk from Lyngby Station. Recent décor, with the emphasis placed on Scandinavian furnishings. Contemporary Danish art brightens up the walls. Comfortable rooms with all facilities. Euro Brasserie Restaurant; Euro Bar and Euro Café. Conference facilities. Golf club, lakes, shops, museums, and other attractions all within easy reach. Private parking. 117 rooms and suites. A few 1- and 2-bedroom apartments.

Hellerup Parkhotel ✻✻ *Strandvejen 203, 2900 Hellerup; Tel. 39 62 40 44, fax 39 62 56 57.* Set in the executive neighbourhood 5 km (3 miles) to the north of central Copenhagen, this is a first-class hotel with every facility, including a health club. Recently refurbished in modern style, the hotel offers a choice of two restaurants, one serving gourmet food, the other Italian. 71 rooms.

Copenhagen

Hotel Hillerød ✹ *Milnersvej 41, 3400 Hillerød; Tel. 48 24 08 00, fax 48 24 08 74.* In the delightful town of Hillerød, the hotel is a mere 40-minute train journey from central Copenhagen. Conveniently situated for exploring the excellent sandy beaches of North Zealand, or for trips farther afield over to Jutland and Sweden. Modern rooms, each with private terrace, bathroom, WC, and kitchenette. 62 rooms in all.

Hotel Prindsen ✹✹ *Algade 13, 4000 Roskilde; Tel. 46 35 80 10, fax 46 35 81 10.* A thoroughly refurbished hotel in the centre of Denmark's oldest royal city, situated about 5 minutes from the cathedral. Friendly atmosphere and efficient service. Restaurant and bar as well as private parking. Children under 12 can stay without charge in their parents' rooms. 46 rooms in all.

Hotel Skandia ✹ *Bramstræde 1, 3000 Helsingør; Tel. 49 21 09 02, fax 49 26 54 90.* An old family-run hotel, just 2 minutes' walk from the railway station. No television or radio in the rooms—helping to retain the authentic atmosphere and rustic charm of this small establishment. All the bedrooms are individually decorated. 43 rooms.

Marienlyst ✹✹ *Nordre Strandvej 2, 3000 Helsingør; Tel. and fax 49 21 40 00.* Well placed for anyone wishing to visit Kronborg. Most rooms have views looking out over the beach and sea. The hotel also has a large restaurant, sauna, and swimming pool. 78 apartments.

Marina ✹✹ *Vedbæk Strandvej 391, 2950 Vedbæk; Tel. 45 89 17 11, fax 45 89 17 22.* Situated midway between Copenhagen and Helsingør, the hotel has stunning views over the harbour and across the Øresund strait to Sweden. All modern facilities are provided for the comfort of guests, including a restaurant (with live music and dancing in the evening), supermarket, sauna, wooded paths for walking and jogging, conference rooms, garage, minibar, and television. There are 127 rooms and 13 apartments.

Recommended Restaurants

With over 2,000 restaurants, many of them serving ethnic cuisine, Copenhagen is something of a gourmet's paradise. Whether you fancy a quick coffee and *wienerbrød* or a five-course feast, you'll have plenty of places to choose from. There are 38 eating establishments alone inside the Tivoli Gardens, while the nearby Scala Centre has numerous bars and restaurants of all types. For lunch, cafés offer the best option for economy-minded diners, with a selection of hot dishes and filling *smørrebrød* at reasonable prices. Dinner can be as light or as heavy as you like, and many places offer traditional Scandinavian open table, where you eat as much as you can for a set charge.

The establishments below are a cross-section of what is available. Prices are based on the cost of a meal per person, including tax but excluding drinks. Note that the high import duty on wine can add considerably to the final bill. For an up-to-date listing of eating establishments, consult the free monthly *Copenhagen This Week* (see page 119).

❀	below 150kr
❀❀	150–300kr
❀❀❀	above 300kr

A Hereford Beefstouw ❀❀ *Vesterbrogade 3, 1620 Copenhagen V; Tel. 33 12 74 41.* Juicy steaks cooked to order near Tivoli Gardens. Open daily from 11:30am to 2pm and 5 to 10:30pm, closed for lunch on the weekend.

Bali ❀❀ *Lille Kongensgade 4, 1074 Copenhagen K; Tel. 33 11 08 08.* On the corner of Kongens Nytorv, offering Indonesian *rijstaffel* and a selection of delicately spiced meat and vegetable dishes. Open daily from noon until midnight.

Copenhagen

Bistro DSB ✿ *Banegårdspladsen 7, 1570 Copenhagen V; Tel. 33 14 12 32.* This railway station restaurant offers a large cold buffet, providing a more than adequate introduction to Danish food. 11:30am to 10pm.

Bøf & Ost ✿ *Gråbrødretorv 13, 1154 Copenhagen K; Tel. 33 11 99 11.* French dishes served with a Danish twist. Open daily from 11:30am to midnight.

Bourgogne ✿✿✿ *Dronningens Tværgade 2, 1302 Copenhagen K; Tel. 33 12 03 17.* In a romantic cellar beneath 300 year-old Moltke Palace. French and Danish cuisine. Open Monday to Saturday from 5pm to 10pm.

Café Sommersko ✿ *Kronprinsessegade 6, 1114 Copenhagen; Tel. 33 14 81 89.* Located just off Strøget, this is a very lively restaurant with a mixed clientele and varied menu, including numerous foreign beers. Open Monday to Wednesday from 9 to 1am, Thursday to Saturday until 2am, and Sunday 10am to 1am.

Cassiopeia ✿✿✿ *Old King Road 10, 1610 Copenhagen; Tel. 33 15 09 33.* A charming lakeside establishment located in the same complex as the planetarium. The restaurant serves a selection of typical Danish cuisine. Open every day from 11:30am until 11pm.

Copenhagen Corner ✿✿ *Rådhuspladsen, 1620 Copenhagen V; Tel. 33 91 45 45.* Excellent food in a restaurant that maintains a traditional atmosphere while serving generally international cuisine. Open every day from 11:30am until midnight.

Den Gule Cottage ✿✿✿ *Strandvejen 506, 2930 Klampenborg; Tel. 39 64 06 91.* French-Danish cuisine served in the attractive setting of a cottage with views on to the sea. Reservations are essential. Open every day from noon to 3:30pm and during the evening 6pm until midnight.

Den Gyldne Fortun ✿✿ *Ved Stranden 18, 1061 Copenhagen K; Tel. 33 12 20 11.* An established fish and shellfish restaurant.

Open Monday to Friday from noon to midnight, weekends from 6pm to 10:30pm.

Divan 1 ✸✸✸ *Vesterbrogade 3, 1620 Copenhagen V; Tel. 33 11 42 42.* One of a wide array of restaurants to be found at Tivoli Gardens, in this case serving mainly international cuisine. Open from the end of April to mid-September daily noon to midnight.

Egoisten ✸✸ *Hovedvagtsgade 2, 1103 Copenhagen K; Tel. 33 12 79 71.* Classic French food and Danish lunch, carefully prepared. Open weekdays noon to midnight; closed weekends.

Els ✸✸✸ *Store Strandstræde 3, 1255 Copenhagen K; Tel. 33 14 13 41.* The elegant 19th-century décor of this delightful restaurant close to Kongens Nytorv complements the stylish cuisine. Fish is a speciality, and the menu changes every day. Reservations are strongly advised.

Færgecaféen ✸ *Strandgade 50, 1401 Copenhagen; Tel. 32 54 46 24.* A little difficult to find, as it is firmly tucked away in Christianshavn (buses 2 and 8), but well worth the effort. A cross between a local bar and a restaurant; possesses a great deal of character. Set menu and à la carte dishes are both available.

Færgen Sjælland ✸✸✸ *Christians Brygge Kajplads 114, 1559 Copenhagen; Tel. 33 13 43 30.* Set on an old ferry moored in the river about half a mile from Rådhuspladsen, this acclaimed restaurant has a number of dining rooms with a range of menus offering mainly international cuisine. Extensive wine list and live entertainment. Open Monday to Thursday noon to midnight, Friday until 1am, Saturday 6pm to 1am.

Ginza ✸✸ *Gammel Kongevej 9, 1610 Copenhagen V; Tel. 31 23 17 46.* Stylishly presented Japanese specialities such as sushi. Open daily noon to 3pm, 5 to 10:30pm, closed for lunch Sunday.

India Palace ✸ *H.C. Andersens Boulevard 13, 1553 Copenhagen V; Tel. 33 91 04 08.* Authentic and tasty Indian cuisine served in pleasant surroundings just a short step from Rådhuspladsen. The restaurant's delicious all-you-can-eat lunch and dinner buffets are extremely popular and excellent value. A la carte dishes also available. Open daily from 11am until midnight.

Klubben ❋ *Enghavevej 4-6, Copenhagen; Tel. 31 24 22 56, 31 31 40 15.* A little out of the way, but well worth a detour. Mixed menu includes a selection of moderately priced dishes, as well as a much cheaper *smørrebrød* menu. Additional attractions include a garden terrace with fishpond and even a small bandstand.

Københavner Caféen ❋ *Badstuestræde 10, 1209 Copenhagen; Tel. 33 32 80 81.* A delightfully typical restaurant situated just off Strøget, particularly recommended for its Danish cold table. Open daily from noon until 10pm.

Kong Hans Kælder ❋❋❋ *Vingårdsstræde 6, 1070 Copenhagen K; Tel. 33 11 68 68.* Top-notch gourmet dining in an attractive vaulted restaurant. The wines are excellent, as are the oysters. Reservations are strongly advised. Open Monday to Saturday from 6pm until 10pm.

Krogs Fiskerestaurant ❋❋❋ *Gammel Strand 38, 1202 Copenhagen K; Tel. 33 15 89 15.* Located in an 18th-century building fitted with early-20th-century décor, this restaurant is justly renowned for its excellent fish dishes. Reservations are strongly recommended. Open Monday to Saturday from 11:30am to 3pm and 5:30 to 10:30pm, but closed on Sunday.

La Mexicana ❋ *Havnegade 47, 1058 Copenhagen K; Tel. 33 11 32 16.* Tequila and tacos in the heart of Denmark. This restaurant offers authentic cuisine in a typically Mexican atmosphere.

Leonore Christine ❋❋❋ *Nyhavn 9, 1051 Copenhagen K; Tel. 33 13 50 40.* Consistently fine gourmet food and attentive service. This restaurant makes a practice of extending an especially warm welcome to foreign visitors. Open daily noon to 3pm and 6pm until midnight.

Le Pavé ❀❀❀ *Gråbrødretorv 14, 1154 Copenhagen; Tel. 33 13 47 45*. French-style cuisine in sophisticated surroundings. Open daily from 11:30am to midnight.

Les Etoiles ❀❀❀ *Dronningens Tværgade 43, 1302 Copenhagen K; Tel. 33 15 05 54*. A restaurant allowing a civilized space between tables, and serving classic French cuisine. Open Tuesday to Friday noon to 3pm, 6pm to 10pm, and Saturday 3pm to 10pm; closed Sunday and Monday.

Lumskebugten ❀❀❀ *Esplanaden 21, 1263 Copenhagen K; Tel. 33 15 60 29*. This small and exclusive restaurant is located by the Churchill Park near the Little Mermaid statue. Outdoor dining. Reservations are essential. Open Monday to Friday from 11am to midnight, Saturday 4pm to midnight.

Mongolian Barbecue ❀ *Stormgade 35, Copenhagen; Tel. 33 14 63 20*. The restaurant provides an excellent-value Mongolian buffet. Open daily from 4pm until midnight.

Nams Kusine ❀❀ *Strandlinien 49, Dragør; Tel. 32 53 18 88*. Situated a little out of the way in the fishing village of Dragør, this delightful restaurant serves fresh seafood with an imaginative flair. The fish soup is highly recommended. Other specialities include succulent chicken roasted in a wood-fired oven. Sea views add to the enjoyable culinary experience. Closed Sunday and Monday.

Nouvelle ❀❀❀ *Gammel Strand 34, 1202 Copenhagen K; Tel. 33 13 50 18*. Equipped with an extensive wine cellar, sommeliers, a Michelin star, and a caviar trolley, this restaurant provides an exquisite location for a special occasion. Unsurprisingly for such an establishment, prices are high. Reservations are essential. Open Monday to Saturday from 11:30am to midnight.

Nyhavns Færgrekro ❀ *Nyhavn 5, 1051 Copenhagen K; Tel. 33 15 15 88*. An unpretentious restaurant serving particularly good traditional food. For lunch an open table with a generous array of fish is set out. Open daily 11:30am to 11:30 pm.

Copenhagen

Pak Ka ✹ *Dronningens Tværgde 30, 1302 Copenhagen K; Tel. 33 15 16 07.* Cantonese cuisine in modern, airy surroundings. Dim sum is served daily (except Thursday) between 11am and 4pm. Open every day from noon until midnight.

Peder Oxe ✹✹ *Gråbrødretorv 11, 1154 Copenhagen K; Tel. 33 11 00 77.* Excellent lunchtime *smørrebrød* offered in a restaurant with a very lively atmosphere. There is also a wine cellar. Open every day from 11:30 to 12:45am.

Rio Bravo ✹✹ *Vestervoldgade 86, 1552 Copenhagen V; Tel. 33 11 75 87.* This is a no-nonsense cowboy-style steakhouse, where even the seats at the bar are saddles. A popular restaurant, and a firm favourite with late-night revellers. Open Monday to Saturday from 12:30pm until 4am, and Sunday from 5pm.

Riz Raz ✹ *Kompagnistræde 20, 1208 Copenhagen K; Tel. 33 15 05 75.* Middle-Eastern buffet-style restaurant; excellent choice for vegetarians. Open daily from 11:30am until midnight.

St. Gertruds Kloster ✹✹✹ *Hauser Plads 32, 1127 Copenhagen K; Tel. 33 14 66 30.* An old monastery is the setting for this gourmet restaurant, which offers a well-stocked wine cellar and elegant menu. Reservations are strongly advised. Open daily from 5 until 11pm.

Shanghai ✹ *Nygade 6 (Strøget), 1164 Copenhagen K; Tel. 33 12 10 01.* Succulent Chinese specialities at reasonable prices. Open from 11:00am until 11:30pm. Also at Scala, Axeltorv 2; tel. 33 15 10 06.

Søllerød Kro ✹✹✹ *Søllerødvej 35, 2840 Holte; Tel. 45 80 25 05.* Good food and a friendly atmosphere in a 17th-century inn. Outdoor dining during the summer. French cuisine with Danish flourishes. Open daily noon to 10pm.

Spisehuset ✹ *Magstrade 12-14, 1466 Copenhagen K; Tel. 33 14 52 70.* Located in Huset, the youth centre (see page 26), the restaurant offers a cheaply priced and pleasantly varied selection of food. Open Tuesday to Saturday from noon to 6pm.